Marcia Langton, AM, is a descendant of the Yiman and Bidjara peoples of Queensland. She was born in Brisbane and raised in small towns, a native camp, and in Brisbane. Since 2000, she has been the Professor of Australian Indigenous Studies at the University of Melbourne, where she teaches and undertakes research on agreements with Indigenous people. She has been a Chief Investigator on several research projects funded by the Australian Research Council resulting in four published collections on agreements with Indigenous people in Australia, New Zealand, North America and South Africa and the online database of agreements with Indigenous people (www.atns.net.au). Her most recent work in this field was edited with Judith Longbottom: *Community Futures, Legal Architecture: Foundations for Indigenous people in the global mining boom*, Routledge (UK), 2012. Her doctoral fieldwork was conducted in eastern Cape York Peninsula during the 1990s, and her experience of the statutory land claim and native title system in this region was informed by a decade of administration and fieldwork pertaining to Aboriginal land rights and Aboriginal deaths in custody in the Northern Territory of Australia. She was awarded a PhD from Macquarie University in

2005. She is a Fellow of the Academy of the Social Sciences of Australia and a member of the Australian Institute of Aboriginal and Torres Strait Islander Studies (AIATSIS). She was Chair of the Cape York Institute for Policy and Leadership from 2004 to 2009.

BOYER
LECTURES
2012

The Quiet Revolution

Indigenous people and the resources boom

BOYER LECTURES

Each year the ABC invites a prominent Australian to present the result of his or her work and thinking on major social, scientific or cultural issues in a series of radio talks known as the Boyer Lectures. The series was inaugurated in 1959 under the title of ABC Lectures, but in 1961 was renamed as a memorial to the late Sir Richard Boyer who, as chairman of the ABC, had been one of those responsible for its introduction.

For further information and for a complete list
of Boyer Lecture speakers visit:
abc.net.au/radionational/boyerlectures

The Boyer Lectures are broadcast each year on ABC Radio National and are available at abc.net.au/radionational/boyerlectures.

ABC Radio National can be found on AM, FM and Digital Radio, and streams live to the world 24/7 via abc.net.au/radionational.

For your local frequency go to abc.net.au/radionational/frequency or call 1300 139 994. Listen online at abc.net.au/radionational.

For ABC Radio National broadcast times and program details go to abc.net.au/radionational or call ABC Radio National listener enquiries on 02 8333 2821.

I am grateful for the assistance of Brigitta Doyle, Mary Rennie and Susan Morris-Yates at ABC Books/HarperCollins, and I would like to thank Julianne Schultz and Peter Robb for their advice. Any errors or omissions in the text are my own.

BOYER
LECTURES
2012

The Quiet Revolution

Indigenous people and the resources boom

Marcia Langton

ABC
Books

The ABC 'Wave' device is a trademark of the Australian Broadcasting Corporation and is used under licence by HarperCollins*Publishers* Australia.

First published in Australia in 2013
by HarperCollins*Publishers* Australia Pty Limited
ABN 36 009 913 517
harpercollins.com.au

Marcia Langton's research has been assisted by a variety of funding sources.
Details: www.sph1.unimelb.edu.au/docs/msph_annual_reports/10_msph_
annual_report.pdf (see page 11)

HarperCollins*Publishers*
Level 13, 201 Elizabeth Street, Sydney NSW 2000, Australia
31 View Road, Glenfield, Auckland 0627, New Zealand
A 53, Sector 57, Noida, UP, India
77–85 Fulham Palace Road, London W6 8JB, United Kingdom
2 Bloor Street East, 20th floor, Toronto, Ontario M4W 1A8, Canada
10 East 53rd Street, New York NY 10022, USA

National Library of Australia Cataloguing-in-Publication entry

Langton, Marcia, 1951–
 The quiet revolution : indigenous people and the resources
 boom / Marcia Langton.
 ISBN: 978 0 7333 3163 3 (pbk.)
 ISBN: 978 1 7430 9912 4 (epub)
 Boyle lectures ; 2012.
 Aboriginal Australians – Economic conditions.
 Mines and mineral resources – Australia.
 Mineral industries – Australia.
 Speeches, addresses, etc., Australian.
305.89915

Cover design by Darren Holt, HarperCollins Design Studio
Image of Peggy Patrick, Argyle Traditional Owner © Argyle Diamonds
Author picture: © Peter Casamento
Typeset in Minion by Kirby Jones

CONTENTS

INTRODUCTION

When I received a letter in June 2012 from the Hon. James Spigelman, AC, QC, Chairman of the Board of the Australian Broadcasting Commission, inviting me to present the fifty-third Boyer Lectures, I felt both honoured and struck with anxiety about the difficulty of condensing my distillation of present thinking about the present circumstances of Aboriginal people. Some of us have stood at the crossroads where it is possible to choose a path to the good life or the path to continuing poverty and marginalisation. Here, some have the capacity to make choices such as education and employment opportunities, for instance. This prestigious lecture series, broadcast on Radio National, could be the perfect opportunity to explain to an important audience ideas and developments in the Aboriginal world that are so poorly represented in the media, in schools and university courses – ideas and developments that have not struck a chord in the public imagination because they contradict a fashionable but outmoded paradigm.

My aim has been to inject new ideas and ways of thinking about the status of Indigenous people in twenty-first century Australia and about the impact of the mining boom in the Aboriginal domain. My hope was that my interpretation of the economic impacts of the boom and some facts about our economic history could be introduced into the national conversation about Aboriginal people, and thereby encourage a more sophisticated view than the archetypal one of the native as perpetual victim with no hope.

Support and appreciation came from my colleagues in the mining and ancillary industries, who are inured to the relentless, tiresome critique, much of it ill informed or downright deceptive, depicting Aboriginal people as the hapless victims of a voracious and brutal mining industry. This view of the mining industry and the Aboriginal engagement with it is at least twenty years out of date. While none of us deny that there are problems still to contend with, and standards to be raised, those of us who negotiate with industry representatives, proposing innovations to improve the situation and to give expression to the rights of Indigenous people, find that one of the obstacles to progress is not the attitudes of people working in the mining industry, but those of the uninformed critics who remain oblivious to the benefits to Aboriginal people from twenty years of operation of the *Native Title Act* and refinements in the implementation of other legislation. It is little known that thousands of jobs for Aboriginal people and hundreds of businesses set up by Aboriginal entrepreneurs are just the tip of the iceberg, and that there have been many other benefits.

Whether I have failed in my goal of changing the narrative from the tired old story of the black victim/ protestor to a more informed account of Aboriginal engagement with modernity, and the resulting cases of economic success and ingenuity against the odds, is a moot question. Have I given those who paid attention pause for thought, a critical interpretation and something more than entertainment? Perhaps these lectures have been a case of too much too soon, given the crazy ideas, hardened attitudes and mythologies about Aboriginal people that abound in Australian society. Or perhaps there is too much invested in the idea of the useless Aboriginal victim to permit, at least in public discourse, that there has been radical change and great progress made. I have pointed to the relatively small but growing number of Aboriginal professionals, experts, businesspeople, artists, filmmakers and sports men and women who have inspired thousands of young Aboriginal people to break the mould and aspire to success.

Those of us who are successful run the risk of being subject to abuse, accused of being 'traitors' to our people, 'assimilationists', and of a number of other crimes against the natural of order of things, as perceived by those who fail to understand their inherited racist worldview. I find myself explaining to young Aboriginal people who find it difficult to understand these opinions that many non-Indigenous people, whether or not they pretend sympathy for the 'Aboriginal problem', in truth prefer their Aborigines to be poor, drunk, drug-addicted or in jail. If you don't conform to this stereotype, then they may accuse you of lying about being Aboriginal 'to obtain benefits'. 'Don't be fooled. Hold your head up,' I say to them, 'and just get on with it. These detractors will never help you and they can only resent your success. They will become increasingly irrelevant as you become more successful.' At least, that is what life has taught me.

The response to these Boyer Lectures has been expressed in a highly polarised debate. This reflects the regular seesawing of opinion about us among the public, influenced by opinion leaders, the media and ideological commitments. This pendulum swings to the rational side of the debate in some circumstances, and then back to the irrational side of the debate. The trick is to catch the swing of opinion at the right moment and inject factual information to encourage sensible and cogent arguments rather than the harebrained ones.

By the very fact of discussing developments in the engagement between Aboriginal people and the mining industry in a compressed history of events, I have flushed out the extremists in the debate. So I want to place the right emphasis on the subject of my lectures here by providing more background to the issues that push the pendulum of public opinion in one direction or the other in relation to the place of Aboriginal people in the nation.

I have endeavoured to explain three key issues in the journey that Aboriginal people have taken from the extreme poverty and marginalisation that was our universal lot in the twentieth century to the much changed situation in the twenty-first century that offers more than a few rungs on the ladder of opportunity to those who choose this path. First, we have many more legal rights and more ability to enjoy these rights than we did fifty years ago. I have focused on native title rights and their impact on our engagement with the mining industry, although there are many others, such as land rights and cultural heritage protection. In the native title field, the negotiation of agreements has been beneficial to hundreds of Aboriginal and Torres Strait Islander groups. There are detriments, but the seat at the table that the right to negotiate provision of the *Native Title Act* has provided gives Aboriginal people the ability to settle many of the conditions of land access, such as jobs, cultural heritage protection and other important matters. Second, the mining industry has changed its *modus operandi* and developed a strategy for involving Aboriginal people in their industry through employment and business opportunities. Like many other Australians, Aboriginal people in the mining industry have increased incomes and a higher standard of living. Third, with important native title rights secured in the twentieth century, Aboriginal people moved quickly to ensure the sustainability of their ancient ways of life and values by dedicating an enormous proportion of their newly returned lands to conservation and biodiversity protection. Largely unnoticed, and especially ignored by aggressively anti-Aboriginal protagonists, is the first Australians' gift to the world: thirty million hectares of their own land designated as protected areas to conserve environments and biodiversity, as discussed in my fourth lecture.

Maintaining our ancient cultural values, and aspects of the old ways of life, is not inimical to economic progress. Aboriginal conservation efforts, particularly in the new 'green' industries, based on partnerships with industry and providing carbon abatement and other services, such as biodiversity surveys by extraordinarily knowledgeable Aboriginal rangers, are examples of the adjustments that Aboriginal groups have made to enable them to keep their traditions and, at the same time, create jobs and businesses to compete in the Australian economy.

None of these three key developments has settled into the public imagination of most Australians, least of all with those of a peculiar leftist persuasion and 'wilderness' campaigners who need Aboriginal people to be powerless victims in their allegorical drama of capitalism in order for their own agendas to make sense.

We reached a critical tipping point some time ago, and those Australians who have helped us reach it understand that Indigenous participation in education systems and the economy are the main pathways out of the miserable conditions that produce ongoing disadvantage and reduce Aboriginal capacity to enjoy their rights as first Australians and citizens of one of the richest nations on earth. This tipping point was reached in progressive steps over a period of many decades. With each government, a few more advances were made. This steady incremental progress has many authors, and my experience is that intelligent, decent people from many walks of life and political persuasions, whether Indigenous people, ministers of the Crown, philanthropists, industry executives, or concerned teachers or workplace supervisors, have contributed something important, no matter how small or how grand. Of course, such people have been members of a tiny minority, and if they were motivated to take action to right an injustice, it was because they were more informed than other Australians, whether through personal effort and inquiry, or by accident. The majority of Australians have remained ignorant of the reasons for the high levels of disadvantage that Indigenous people face, both because the reasons are complex, and because there is a wealth of disinformation as well as irrational belief about Aboriginal people in circulation.

No one political party has ownership rights on 'doing the right thing'. I take no sides in the political landscape, carved up as it is by parties and movements. The truth is always much more complicated than the policy positions of governments, parties and campaign offices would have us believe.

In the last twenty years, four prime ministers have presided over policies and programs in Indigenous affairs, including the recognition of native title, and each of them has, among all the political machinations, taken a step in the right direction, sometimes reluctantly, and sometimes enthusiastically. The recognition of native title was unimaginable a quarter of a century ago.

Koiki Eddie Mabo left an extraordinary legacy, not simply because his court case overturned 200 years of the legal fiction that had resulted in the dispossession of Aboriginal people around Australia, but also because it paved the way for the development of legislation which, if properly used, has the capacity to provide economic opportunity for Indigenous communities.

According to the context and the relative situation of Indigenous parties, choosing whether to pursue native title outcomes through litigation or negotiated settlement can be a very delicate challenge.[1] Many native title claims have failed. Litigation in the current judicial climate is not always an effective means by which to achieve beneficial outcomes for Indigenous people. Some Aboriginal people and their representatives involved in the native title system have chosen to negotiate rather than litigate, when the opportunity presents itself.[2]

Progress is often slow, and state governments and their solicitors aggressively adversarial, yet many positive outcomes can be discerned on the chequerboard of native title claims and court-determined areas across the continent. Agreement outcomes are generating significant benefits for the negotiating parties, securing land access for project rights,[3] employment opportunities,[4] and cultural heritage protection, as well as establishing regimes for the management of natural resources.[5]

A deeper understanding of the issues has caused some mining companies to change their attitudes to the issues of mining impacts and the entitlement of Aboriginal communities to benefits as a result of the detriment they incur from mining and related activities.[6] The Minerals Council of Australia has explicitly expressed a preference for the negotiation of a sustainable relationship, with agreed approaches to, and the conditions for, land access and local support for mining operations as a more successful strategy.[7] This strategy is subtly different from the conventional corporate social responsibility approach, defined by the World Business Council for Sustainable Development as 'the continuing commitment by business to behave ethically and contribute to economic development while improving the quality of life of the workforce and their families as well as of the local community and society at large'.[8] There is more than one motivation for mining companies to reach agreement with local traditional Aboriginal owners: to avoid costly litigation and delays to exploration and mining projects is a practical reason.[9] There is also a growing recognition in the mining industry that 'it will be increasingly difficult for them to operate profitably unless they establish cooperative working relationships with local indigenous interests'.[10]

More needs to be done in the policy arena to create an enabling economic environment for Aboriginal people.

In the last twenty years, the sophistication of our thinking around how these provisions might translate into economic and social opportunity has increased significantly. Economic participation and wealth creation at far higher levels than twenty years ago are the two outstanding outcomes of the Right to Negotiate. Yet as more and more resource companies and Indigenous communities sit together at the negotiating table, we must continue to build on the legacy of Mabo and ensure the benefits of agreements can be fully realised, for this generation and the next. The ability of native title groups to join the economy and achieve parity is at stake.

Support in sections of the Australian mining industry for procedural fairness in dealing with our native title rights is now secure, but these rights have come under attack from other quarters.

In these lectures, I also aimed to correct or raise some doubts about the veracity of the 'wilderness' campaigners' stance towards Aboriginal people, which relegates us to the status of the 'new noble savage' and enemies of their grand struggle to save nature. I had hoped, especially in my fourth Boyer Lecture, that I had distinguished clearly between 'wilderness' campaigners and the scientists who have collaborated intelligently with Aboriginal conservation workers. Such distinctions fell on deaf ears. Some raised an old furphy. In 1994, Tim Flannery published his speculation that the first Australians, some thousands of years ago, were responsible for the extinction of the Australian megafauna. Several scientists have dismissed his claim, as did I.[11] His highly speculative theory has been damaging to Aboriginal people, particularly because it has become the 'respectable' source for hateful claims made by racists in the 'green' movement, advocates for Indigenous genocide, and among grazier activists intent on turning back Aboriginal rights. In 2012, while I was finalising a lecture, Flannery claimed in his *Quarterly Essay: After the Future, Australia's New Extinction Crisis* that:

> … mining often takes priority over nature protection. Even under Labor governments with a strong green bent, *national parks are not always safe* [my emphasis]. In 2010, the Queensland Bligh government began the process of de-gazetting a large part of Mungkan Kaanju National Park on Cape York Peninsula, with a view to giving the land back to its traditional Aboriginal owners.[12]

I deal with the implications of this message in the fourth chapter, including the potential to read it as opposition to recognising Aboriginal rights in land, although it should be noted Flannery has publicly denied this interpretation of his essay.[13] I went on to explain the history of that national park and Aboriginal stewardship of Australian environments in the last two decades including, as I have said, the designation of thirty million hectares of their own land as protected areas to conserve environments and biodiversity. This is surely a win for all Australians.

The evidence against Flannery's speculation comes from a number of disciplines; much of it is published in specialist refereed journals and a few books, and much of it relates, ironically, to climate change, especially the drying up of the Australian continent during the Tertiary Period. Along with the conflation of early human populations with modern Aboriginal populations in his book, there are examples of indiscriminate and incorrect use of evidence of vegetation change as a result of fire from one era applied to another era, when there is no firm chronology of either climatological or human impacts. There are examples of the indiscriminate and incorrect use of evidence from temperate regions applied to the wet–dry tropics.

Widely but mistakenly accepted by his lay readership as an account of settled scientific opinion, Flannery's argument is ingenious and seductive.

It is the seemingly logical order of six improbable events based on unproven claims about fire, the first

Australians, flora and fauna from the Pleistocene to the British colonial period that is so superficially attractive, but also improbable, because, as I have said, he has aligned slight and miscellaneous fragments of evidence from vastly different periods across many thousands of years and arranged them into a neat fictional order. The archaeological reconstruction of the chronology, distribution and movement of human groups over the continent in the last 60,000 years is largely guesswork and, consequently, we can only speculate as to the cause and effect of burning and vegetation change which might have resulted from such human activity. Aborigines have become a panacaea which other palaeoecological disciplines can apply to salve their otherwise intractable problems, particularly their inability to solve particular questions about the degree of human responsibility for the effect of fire on ancient landscapes. That is difficult because of the extreme climatic variation and gradual drying of the continent since the Tertiary.

Botanist D.M.J.S. Bowman, employed by the Parks and Wildlife Commission of the Northern Territory in 1994, was one who refuted Flannery's speculative hypothesis in his Tansley Review in *New Phytologist*, remarking that this was a 'simple caricature'. Bowman concluded that there is insufficient evidence to support the speculative hypotheses that Aboriginal landscape burning was primarily responsible for the extinction of Pleistocene megafauna and other claims made by Flannery. He explained that:

> 'The question of the original impact of humans on the Australian environment is fundamentally speculative because of the vague and disputed time frames proposed for the waves of colonisation and shifting settlement patterns of Aborigines in the late Quaternary.' [14]

The speculative hypotheses of Flannery and others are based on a circularity of argument concerning the cause and effect of climate change, vegetation change and burning through the late Quaternary period. Flannery had strayed far beyond his disciplinary boundaries and area of expertise, and the experts with a profound knowledge of these matters could do little to correct the mistaken view that he had foisted onto a gullible public.

Flannery's argument, as debatable as it is, has been much used and much misrepresented by non-expert environmentalists, graziers and other Australians looking for support for their racist beliefs, and seeking to assert their purportedly superior custodianship of the Australian continent. In the late 1990s, the New South Wales Grazier's Association published a guide for its members relying heavily on Flannery's hypothesis to reassure them that, given the purported Aboriginal destruction of early Pleistocene environments and, as it is further purported, the resulting demise of the megafauna in a 'single extinction event', modern Australian pastoralism constitutes restoration of the Australian environment. Flannery's theory is a misuse of a tendentious and difficult theoretical proposition that is scientifically unsustainable.

I have indicated how the pendulum of opinion on matters relating to Aboriginal people swings. There will be more swings from one extreme to another, because of the emotional and intellectual impact of our continuing existence in Australian society. It is clearly difficult for many Australians to come to terms with us, with our shared history and with the challenges of Aboriginal adjustments to modernity. The historical burden of the dispossession and maltreatment of Indigenous people is just as troublesome for many settler and immigrant Australians as it is for Aboriginal people.

Unlike those who prefer fantasies about the Aboriginal world, there are those who have engaged directly with Aboriginal people and participated in the extraordinary changes of the last twenty years. Whether Indigenous or not, they come from many backgrounds: some are native title lawyers, others mining company executives and employees, and yet others are philanthropists, researchers or Aboriginal business owners. They too have observed the changes I describe in these Boyer Lectures. There is more work to be done getting young Aboriginal people educated, work-ready and into careers to enable them to enjoy living standards that most Australians take for granted. I have given my own account and interpretation of the political and policy history and issues that help or hinder in these goals. We are making some headway, and it is vital that more Aboriginal people come to understand the futility of some political or ideological stances.

I am grateful for the responses from the many who argued reasonable points with my contentions; it was such debates that I hoped would ensue from the lectures. The role of a public intellectual is not to agree with the paradigm but to be sceptical, to ask questions, refute mistaken beliefs, discuss important ideas and literature, provide accurate information and cogent interpretations of matters. If my Boyer Lectures have met these standards and lead to a more informed debate and better understanding of the Aboriginal situation, they have served their purpose.

ONE

FAUSTIAN BARGAIN OR SURVIVAL STRATEGY? MINING AND ABORIGINAL ECONOMIC EMPOWERMENT

The emergence of an Aboriginal middle class in Australia in the last two to three decades has gone largely unnoticed.[1] While the numbers remain small, this change heralds an economic future for Aboriginal people unimaginable fifty years ago. When in 1968 W.E.H. Stanner delivered the Boyer Lectures – *After the Dreaming: Black and white Australians – An anthropologist's view* – he gave credence, perhaps inadvertently, to the then widely held assumption that Aboriginal life was incompatible with modern economic life.[2] Today, the expectation is quite the reverse.

The policies of federal governments for the last decade have implied, and increasingly made explicit, the expectation that educational achievement and employability will be the key outcomes of spending in Indigenous Affairs portfolios. This is a view generally shared by most ordinary Australians.

But on the left, and among those opinion leaders who hang on to the idea of the 'new noble savage', Aboriginal poverty is invisible, masked by their 'wilderness' ideology.[3] They describe the Aboriginal situation through a romantic lens. Their unspoken expectation is that no Aboriginal group should become engaged in any economic development. I will return to these matters of Aboriginal poverty, welfare dependency and the 'wilderness' campaigns against economic development in the following lectures.

By the late 1980s, Indigenous policy and much public commentary in Australia was based on a paradigm which cast Aboriginal people as victims of a brutal colonial legacy, as residents of remote regions where they strove to maintain the vestiges of a traditional way of life, an endeavour in which they needed the support of government through income assistance schemes and other policies that would help them to stay on their traditional lands. Over the following two decades this paradigm came under increasing attack, led by Noel Pearson, on the grounds that it fundamentally misunderstood the nature of contemporary Aboriginal life in Australia, the problems facing Aboriginal people and appropriate policy responses.

Indigenous people came to be treated, not just as different, but exceptional, and inherently incapable of joining the Australian polity and society. The history of legislation and policy applied to Indigenous people demonstrates this in a number of ways: not citizens until after the 1967 Referendum; the shameful effects of the nearly half-century-old Community Development Employment Program (a work-for-the dole scheme); entrenchment of Aboriginal people in welfare dependency; and the Northern Territory Emergency Intervention; all these exceptionalist initiatives have isolated the Aboriginal world from Australian economic and social life. The Mabo case, the *Native Title Act* and engagement with the mining industry have changed the assumptions of that paradigm and catapulted Aboriginal people engaged in the mining industry into the mainstream economy. I have worked at mine sites and witnessed this extraordinary change.

The Argyle Diamond Mine is the world's largest producer of diamonds. It sits atop and eastwards of a dramatic red mountain range to the southwest of the Ord River Dam in the east Kimberley region of Western Australia. I have often approached it from the southwest, driving back from the Warmun Aboriginal community. The mine pit breaks the horizon with a sharp V cut into the ridgeline. The old Aboriginal women, who know the story and care about this place, with a vigilant regard for even the mine itself, look at it and think of the ever-present Barramundi woman Daiwul, just below the haul trucks circling down the huge excavation.

When I first went to the east Kimberley in 1980, I was deeply shocked at the poverty and racism that seemed then to be the unalterable fate of the Aboriginal people living in Kununurra, Warmun (or Turkey Creek, as it was known then) and the stock camps. Cruel, hard white men ruled the region, and their behaviour towards Aboriginal people was malevolent, random and without cause.

Still today, for most Aboriginal people there, life is hard, very hard.

My first visit to the Argyle Diamond Mine was in early 2000 when Rio Tinto Ltd was moving towards buying out the other shareholders. At that time, there were four Aboriginal employees. Two of them were gardeners. Two years later, there were many more. Among the people who made this change, giving jobs to local Aboriginal people, was the mine manager, Brendan Hammond, recently arrived from Namibia, and originally from the former Rhodesia, now Zimbabwe. Like other southern Africans, he had lived through the dismantling of apartheid and the independence movement in his own country as well as Namibia and Angola. He told me he was shocked at the racism in Australia, and that what he was dealing with in the vicinity of the mine was worse than anything he had encountered at home. The new Rio Tinto policy framework for engaging with Aboriginal people with respect for their rights gave him an extraordinary opportunity. He gave a direct order to the community relations staff to ensure that more Aboriginal people were employed. I attended a meeting with the staff of the mine in 2001, when discussions had commenced in earnest to identify jobs for Aboriginal people. With an undertone of aggression, a man said, 'We can't employ Aboriginal people because they have got problems with alcohol and they all have police records. This is a high-security site. It wouldn't work.' Some shuffled subtly in their chairs and must have felt embarrassed. Those who knew of the instruction from the manager must have been wondering, 'How indeed would this work?' I said, 'The best thing to do would be to employ Aboriginal women. They don't have problems with alcohol or the police.' The response was a thick silence; but one man, the late Fred Murray, had a twinkle in his eye. When I next visited the mine, he made a great fuss about meeting me at the security gate. The security team was a group of tough local Aboriginal women, and Fred's face beamed with pride. Later, I learnt that they had busted the local police leaving the mine site for a weekend in Kununurra. They were caught with company bed linen in the boot of their police vehicle.

Brendan Hammond became a champion for the Aboriginal people of the east Kimberley. He revolutionised the culture of the Argyle Diamond Mine by opening the doors to Aboriginal people. Today, the rate of Aboriginal employment at that mine stands at 25 per cent of the total workforce. This remarkable change in the employment of Aboriginal people on mining projects accelerated throughout the first decade of this century. But is it threatened by the downturn in the mining sector, dependent as it is on China's demand for Australian resources?

* * *

In this lecture, I want to examine some of the significant changes in the Aboriginal world due in some part to the present boom in the mining industry. This story of the Aboriginal part in Australia's economic history begins in the protection era and ends as the mining boom collides with the Aboriginal remote world and incoherent government policies on Aboriginal economic development. Mining offers many Indigenous populations a significant source of employment and contracting opportunities, as an alternative to the state subsidies, such as social security and other Commonwealth funding transfers, upon which many remote and regional Aboriginal communities depend.[4]

We have a responsibility to ensure that what happens next is not a social and economic disaster for Aboriginal people. To do so, we need to understand the forces at work; the factors, historical and economic, that have produced the present situation.

Most people are ignorant about Aboriginal economic history, and, in particular, how recently Aboriginal people began to join the economy, moving from indentured and unfree labour status to full economic participation.

In the 1960s laws changed.[5] The 1967 Referendum on constitutional inclusion of Aboriginal people moved the policy momentum along, capturing the spirit of most Australians that demanded equal treatment and a fair go. Aboriginal people began to migrate from reserves, rural towns and fringe camps to the cities.

Aboriginal people entered the cash economy in greater numbers and more rapidly than ever before. In increasing numbers, and for the first time, they enjoyed the political and economic fruits of Australian citizenship: the social welfare safety net, some aspects of economic development, political representation, support for language and culture, and government policy and funding to improve outcomes in health, education and sports.

Since the late 1990s, the private sector, especially the resource extraction industries, has set bold Indigenous employment targets and, to meet them, provided on-the-job training, contracting and procurement practices to ensure that Aboriginal people and their enterprises succeed.

There are hundreds of Aboriginal businesses, and even more Aboriginal not-for-profit corporations, with income streams, delivering economic outcomes to their communities on an unprecedented scale.

In the last decade, mining companies and ancillary services have employed Aboriginal and Torres Strait

Islanders in larger numbers than ever before in Australian history. Some mining companies, for example Rio Tinto Ltd, Fortescue Metals Group and BHP Billiton, have developed recruitment and other labour force strategies in the last few years that have contributed to the creation of the largest Australian Indigenous industrial workforce ever. In mid 2011, in the Pilbara alone, Rio Tinto Iron Ore had over a thousand Indigenous employees, and Fortescue more than three hundred. As proportions of the total workforce in both these companies, about eight per cent of the employees are Indigenous. Nationally, Rio Tinto has about 1500 Indigenous employees.

These and other companies, such as Woodside Energy, are also offering Indigenous entrepreneurs unprecedented opportunities to tender for contracts. Rio Tinto Iron Ore Ltd and Fortescue awarded more than $300 million in 2011 to Indigenous contracting companies in the Pilbara. Both companies exceeded this contract spending on Aboriginal enterprises in 2012. In 2011, it was estimated that there were fifty-two contracting companies owned by Indigenous businesses or in joint ventures with Indigenous companies that had successfully tendered for Rio Tinto Iron Ore contracts. These companies are also employing Indigenous people at an unprecedented rate.

Yet continuing high levels of disadvantage remain, even among Indigenous populations located near resource projects. It is vital that we understand the constraints on Indigenous economic participation.

In the following lecture, I will examine the underbelly of the resources boom and in subsequent lectures the standing of the Indigenous population in the Australian economy – especially those who live in northern Australia and the remote regions that form the geographic heart of this activity.

Mining is the only significant industry in remote communities, and dependence on it may leave these communities in a precarious position when an operation closes. High levels of dependency on mining can be detrimental to Indigenous and rural and regional communities, so development aimed at increasing economic diversity becomes necessary. And now that there is talk that the resources boom has peaked, how vulnerable to the mining downturn are these Aboriginal businesses?

Many of Australia's largest mines are in very remote areas, with substantial Indigenous populations living nearby. Once a battleground between Aboriginal people fighting for basic rights against ruthless mining corporations unfettered by legislative protection of the local people or the environment, an accord has been reached in many areas where native title rights have provided the leverage for negotiated settlements.

Historically the mining sector had a poor record of Indigenous employment and this has led to the mistaken assumptions that Indigenous people were not interested in working in the mining industry and were unable to acquire the skills to do so.

Earlier this year Matthew Gray, Research Fellow at the Centre for Aboriginal Economic Policy Research (CAEPR) at the Australian National University, and I addressed the question: 'What has changed?' We found that there were three factors which made this mining boom different and opened up the possibility of economic benefit flowing for the first time to local people who live near the sites of these mines.

First, the current mining boom is very large. According to Treasury, in 2010 about 27,000 jobs were created in the mining industry. It looks probable that the boom will continue for a number of years, with large projects either underway or planned. Mines now being developed will create many more jobs and their economic benefits will flow on to regional centres.

Second, the boom has taken place during a period of very strong growth in the whole economy. The resulting tight labour market has meant that mining companies have had trouble finding employees. Many Australians don't want to work in the remotest areas of Australia, and often must do so on a fly-in fly-out basis.[6]

Third, mining companies are increasingly realising that Indigenous employment is an important part of agreements to mine on Indigenous land. It maintains the companies' 'social licence' to mine. Companies with many Indigenous employees have often made significant investments in recruiting and training them. A few companies have provided programs to ensure standards of literacy and numeracy compliant with industry norms, to support families and communities, and to mentor Indigenous employees. These have all been critical to increasing Indigenous employment. Fortescue Metals Group guarantees employment and home ownership to members of the traditional owner groups that have signed land access agreements and completed training courses provided by its Vocational Training and Education Centre. Companies have often increased cultural awareness within their workplaces and reduced discrimination.

While these programs involve costs to mining companies, the companies have found that the business case stacks up. Outside the mining industry, more

Indigenous people have also been finding work in the economy as a whole.

The recent increases in Indigenous employment in the mining industry have occurred in the context of substantial increases in Indigenous employment since the mid 1990s. Between 1994 and 2008, Indigenous employment increased from about thirty per cent of Indigenous people of working age to about half of that population set in the national workforce. Much of this growth was in the private sector.[7]

A number of factors have contributed to these increases since the early 1990s recession. Key among them are the strong macro economy, which has created many new jobs, and the combined efforts of government, community organisations and the private sector to increase the skill level and employability of Indigenous Australians.

The mining industry has created opportunities to make enduring inroads into the gap in employment rates between Indigenous and other Australians, and it has established a model for expanding these opportunities across Australian society. Achieving this will require significant investment and commitments from both the private sector and governments. This will be crucial to the economic success and social stability of Australia in the Asian Century. Maintaining the gains and the momentum of change brought by the resources boom could be transformative.

The demographic profile of regional and remote Aboriginal populations is overwhelmingly young: their future depends on their inclusion in the economy through education and work. The young age profile of the Indigenous population – approximately 58 per cent of the Indigenous population is under the age of twenty-five – means that large numbers of young people will reach working age over the next decade. Australia cannot afford for this group of young people to be excluded from the benefits of paid employment as many of their parents were. For the first time, there are now large numbers of good, well-paying jobs to be had in remote Australia.

Yet the responsibility for encouraging and funding education, health services, housing, and other basic infrastructure lies with state and territory governments – which have historically neglected, and continue to neglect, the citizens of remote Australia, especially Aboriginal peoples. As John Taylor, director of CAEPR at the Australian National University, and Ben Scambary, head of the Aboriginal Areas Protection Authority (AAPA) in the Northern Territory, reminded us in 2005, 'Despite unprecedented labour demand … the capacity of local Indigenous people to benefit remains substantially constrained by their limited human capital'.[8]

As Australia's resources boom has waxed and waned, the effects on Indigenous people have been mixed. Scores of mines have opened or expanded in the last decade, but in the last two years, with the economic downturn in China, a few major expansions and projects have been delayed or closed, such as at Olympic Dam in South Australia.

Are we now in danger of losing the economic gains – many driven, as we can see, by the private sector – of the last fifty years? How will our way of life change as skilled workers are imported to cope with the domestic shortages? As the baby boomer generation retires, how will our cultures change?[9]

These questions loom large as governments and the finance sector come to terms – rather late in the piece – with the needs of the new Indigenous entrepreneurs. Governmental policy settings have been frozen for a long time in the apologetic 1970s view of the Aboriginal world. Now, almost fifty years after the first wave of reforms to the legal and political treatment of Aboriginal people, the present stasis in Indigenous policy threatens the fragile achievements of Aboriginal workers and business people by locking them out of the economy with few incentives for participation and many disincentives. It is difficult to see how the federal policy on Indigenous economic development is of any help in overcoming welfare dependency.

Government policies, media reportage and public attitudes have barely registered the extraordinary changes in the Aboriginal world of the last half century. One of the most important is that demographic and regional change in Aboriginal Australia in that period has been remarkable, with a growing difference between Indigenous populations of the south and those of the north. By 2040, half the population of northern Australia will be Indigenous; in the south, it will remain at about 2 or 3 per cent.

In 2012, Indigenous people own 82 per cent of northern Australia in a variety of titles: pastoral leases, freehold leases, native title determinations, and special Aboriginal freeholds, which include reserves converted to trust arrangement and areas returned following successful land claims. Aboriginal pastoral properties are the second largest type of land holding. Thus the economic interests of Indigenous and non-Indigenous people in northern Australia are closely aligned – mining, cattle, tourism are the industries that fuel the northern economy. There, the predominant issues raised by Aboriginal advocates concern land acquisition, industry and commerce, education, training, employment and health issues.

In the south, however, the predominant issues raised in the media and public domain by Aboriginal advocates, are not so practical. Rather they concern human rights, reconciliation and 'self-determination'. Issues such as education, employment and health take second place.

The rapid, if dispersed, industrialisation of remote Australia is changing the traditional balance of power between the cities and the bush.

What will be urban Australia's response to the Aboriginal north? These are the questions I have asked myself, standing at the edge of a mine pit in remote Australia, peering over the edge.

It is likely that the people of the outback will be less the stubborn, deprived victims of Pauline Hanson's imagination, and more the avant-garde of a wealthy remote-area workforce.

The shift of infrastructure from the east coast to the remote inland and west is striking. Most Australians live in cities far away from the mining provinces, so they are unlikely ever to see the absurd contrast between the primitive mining towns of the past and new modern-day versions. They are also largely unaware of the great wealth these new communities generate, or even the nature of twenty-first century industrial mining – the automation, the giant machinery and the capital-intense way that minerals are now extracted from the ground. The reality is that since 1967 the mining industry has built twenty-six towns, twelve ports (and additional bulk handling infrastructure at many existing ports), twenty-five airfields, and over 2000 kilometres of railway line. An economic and cultural shift is happening in the inland, and it barely registers in the big cities.

It seems that the mining and allied metal industries are constantly the battleground of public dramas. Indeed, this has been so since colonial times. In 1963, Geoffrey Blainey named one of his most popular books, in which he reinterpreted the Eureka rebellion, *The Rush That Never Ended*. The goldfields societies formed the cauldron in which modern Australia brewed. It was gold that brought people to Australia and paid for banks and shops and towns to be built. The lust for gold was responsible for an extraordinary population growth.

The Ophir gold rush in 1851 was only the second major gold rush in the world after the one that began in California 1848, and attracted prospectors from all over the globe to the central west of New South Wales. In 1852 alone, 370,000 immigrants arrived in Victoria, and in just two years the state's population grew from 77,000 to 540,000, and by 1871 to 1.7 million. Bathurst in New South Wales, and Ballarat and Bendigo in Victoria, and a few other towns, survived the gold rushes as thriving rural communities, but most did not. Many, such as Cooktown in Cape York, or Pine Creek in the Northern Territory, are now quiet backwaters. There are ghost towns scattered across the country.

Mostly, though, the small outback towns are now Aboriginal communities, as generation after generation from the old white families moved to the cities. The demographic of the remote inland is becoming a majority Aboriginal world, broken up by islands of mine workers and a few service centres.

After World War II, geologists and others, such as Lang Hancock, discovered a series of gargantuan ore bodies. These discoveries – iron ore in the Pilbara in 1952, and bauxite in Arnhem Land in 1950 and Cape York in 1955, for instance – heralded two developments in Australia: a vast expansion of industrial-scale mining by corporations and conflict with local Aboriginal groups.

Whereas gold mining in the nineteenth century had been largely artisanal, with diggers pitching their tents amid the anarchy of the early goldfields, a different scale of mining, such as commenced at Broken Hill in the 1880s and at Mt Isa in the 1920s, represented the beginnings of the corporate mining industry that is driving the resources sector today. In the nineteenth century and for much of the twentieth century, mine operators and governments paid little regard to the detrimental impact of mining operations on neighbouring Indigenous people. Indeed, governments often removed Aboriginal people from these areas to allow the unimpeded establishment and continuation of the mines.

In 1963 this began to change with a campaign that joined Aboriginal people with churches, unions and international groups to protest at the treatment of Aboriginal people by the Queensland government and the mining company Comalco Pty Ltd. The Queensland police burnt down the houses and church of the Aboriginal community living at the Mapoon mission, and forcibly relocated the residents to New Mapoon. It was clear that the government's intention was to remove the community to allow the unimpeded development of the bauxite mine at Weipa.[10]

Only an official apology by Peter Beattie, former Premier of Queensland, and the successful negotiation of the Comalco Western Cape Communities Coexistence Agreement with the Wik and other peoples in 2001 have overcome the legacy of these activities by government and police.

In 1963 in the Northern Territory, in northeast Arnhem Land, a bauxite mining operation was imposed on the Yolngu people, who litigated and resisted for another forty years.[11]

These and similar events have had lasting implications for relations between the Indigenous people and the mining industry. Several Aboriginal land councils were formed to prevent further incidents and to obtain recognition of their rights to their traditional lands and to prevent mining companies from proceeding without their approval: the North Queensland Land Council was formed in 1977; then, in 1978, elders and traditional owners established the Kimberley Land Council in Western Australia; and later, the Cape York Land Council was formed in 1990.

But this is to anticipate the advent of the recognition of native title. Throughout the mining boom of the

1960s and 1970s, other similar events took place. And in the 1980s, conflicts with Aboriginal people exploded. At Noonkanbah in the Kimberley in 1980 the mining industry was pitted against Aboriginal people who were seeking to protect a sacred site. The West Australian government ordered the drilling of the site by Amax Pty Ltd to pursue mineral exploration objectives, and was prepared to support it against the protests with large numbers of police.

An international campaign protesting the desecration of Aboriginal sacred sites damaged the reputation of the mining industry. And with this, the standing of the industry changed. Whereas previously few questions had been asked about the way the industry operated, and governments had encouraged the opening of new mining operations and exploration because of the contribution to economic growth, concerns were now being raised that caught the public imagination throughout the world, as protests were delivered to national and international forums.

A view of the mining industry emerged among its critics that forced the industry to rethink its relationship with Australian Indigenous people. The rights of Indigenous people, the preservation of cultural heritage, environmental management, and the reputation of Australia as a first-world nation with a fourth-world underclass suffering at the hands of the mining industry: all of these issues troubled those Australians who wanted a better deal for Indigenous people. Some in the mining industry and in government were sceptical about the purpose of what they saw as the 'politics of embarrassment', yet the incentives for the mining industry to build and maintain distinctive internal capabilities – such as the ability to handle and resolve social issues to maintain their mandate – grew, and this involved reconsidering their relationships with Indigenous people.

Commonwealth recognition of Aboriginal rights to land in the Northern Territory coincided with an earlier, smaller mining boom in the 1960s and 1970s. Lobbyists in the mining industry held that Aboriginal responses to the many proposals for exploration and mining were unreasonable because they were different from conventional arrangements with landowners and others who were affected by the industry. The industry bodies of the day also insisted that Aboriginal objections to the encroachment of mining operations into their domain were holding back economic development in Australia, with the result that Aboriginal people were demonised by the industry. Gloomy investor forecasts contributed to the hateful attitudes towards Indigenous people of that time. Some feared that a future of open-ended land claims would limit exploration and expansion of the mining industry, and that the new land rights legislated for Aboriginal people would lead to unsustainable legal and financial consequences.

But when mining company employees began to explore the reasons for Aboriginal opposition to mining in the 1980s, they discovered that many Aboriginal groups were not opposed to mining itself, but were concerned about the racist and inequitable situation of the past being replicated and consolidated in new ventures.

It was widely assumed that Aboriginal people were making ambit claims for land and financial returns to which they were not entitled, and many in the mining industry treated Aboriginal objections to mining proposals with contempt. The state governments had dealt with Aboriginal demands in less than constructive ways, which further hindered the possibility of mining companies and Aboriginal groups talking about the issues constructively.

Aboriginal people were opposed to the potential for worsening racial discrimination and abuse that so often accompanied mining projects imposed on them by state governments (such as occurred with the 1957 *Comalco Act* in western Cape York). They wanted guaranteed recognition of their inherent rights and entitlements, and acceptable terms and conditions for their cultural, social and economic futures.

At that time, legislation requiring the mining industry to consult with Aboriginal people about mining proposals either did not exist in most states, or, where the *Aboriginal Land Rights Act* had been introduced – in the Northern Territory – the mining provisions had not been tested. The mining industry in Western Australia, where there were no Aboriginal rights, was expanding, with the Pilbara mining operations growing, and companies exploring for diamonds in the Kimberley and for uranium in the Western Desert.

Indigenous people feared that their cultural heritage would be destroyed, the environment degraded, and that their rights and interests as traditional owners would be lost, as more and more leases were obtained by mining companies. In making their objections, Indigenous people were fulfilling their customary responsibilities to 'look after country' and to protect and promote their cultural integrity and social vitality. They had good reasons for these fears. Historically, mining companies had long discriminated against Aboriginal people, and there was little evidence that companies would provide employment for local Indigenous people. It was the High Court's Mabo decision on 3 June 1992 that changed this history of conflict.

The twentieth anniversary of the Mabo decision in the High Court was celebrated throughout Australian Indigenous communities in 2012. Mabo's legacy is profound. Although not anticipated at the time, the Mabo decision and the *Native Title Act* of 1993 provided a formal place at the table for Aboriginal people. Those newly won native title rights placed them in a key position with companies seeking land access issues in the market economy.[12]

Aboriginal people have used the 'Right to Negotiate' to negotiate agreements for access to their land to great advantage, settling many thousands of agreements with mining companies and other resource-extraction companies. There is no right of veto, but a seat at the table. This is where ingenuity and leadership counts. These agreements, such as between the Wik people of western Cape York and Comalco, amount to a bargain between Indigenous peoples and the mining companies, producing income streams which – in the best circumstances – could accumulate several billions of dollars for future generations, along with jobs and enterprise development, in return for the impacts of mining.[13]

By translating the recognition of their native title into tangible economic and social benefits for their communities, native title groups have achieved far higher levels of economic participation and wealth creation through employment and enterprise development.

The challenges that lie ahead, however, are complex. If I were to describe them in one phrase, it would be 'economic empowerment'. How do we unlock the economic potential of these mining agreements? The answer, in one sentence, would be: if Aboriginal people had access to jobs, and communities had access to genuine economic and investment advice and equality in education and training, this would enable Aboriginal people to participate in the marketplace and to accumulate wealth. Some Aboriginal assets would be converted to commercial assets with income streams. If this were to come about, there would be no 'gap'; no alarming rates of disadvantage for Aboriginal people across most of the socioeconomic indicators. Some thousands of Aboriginal men and women working in the mining and other industries have imagined this future for themselves and have achieved it. Why not all Aboriginal people? This – a rather large question with many facets – will be addressed in the coming lectures.

TWO

IN FROM THE COLD: THE
EMERGENCE OF THE ECONOMIC
ABORIGINE

Twenty-five years ago, a mobile population of used-car dealers, grog runners, hire-purchase loan sharks, boosters for mining and exploration, and fundamentalist Christians drifted through the towns and Aboriginal communities of Australia's remote areas. The used-car dealers sold Aboriginal people decrepit second-hand cars for prices ranging from 2000 to 10,000. They made enormous profits and added to the strata of racist mythology and hatred. They were welcomed by Aboriginal people – who were unaware of their predicament as a targeted, vulnerable market – into their communities throughout the Central Desert when royalty cheques were due. After their visits, happy owners of these wrecks drove them for a month at best, and a couple of days at worst, before they ended up parked, permanently, by the side of the road leading to the community. Many of the now-rusted car bodies remain there still, exactly where they stopped years ago, along the roads that cross the deserts from Kalgoorlie and Kununurra in Western Australia, from Adelaide in South Australia, from Darwin in the Top End, and Camooweal in Queensland. When word reached the spivs in the big cities of the thousands of dollars to be made, more came with cargoes of cars loaded up on big trucks, and set up pop-up car yards opposite the Aboriginal organisations that paid out the royalty cheques. They even flew Aboriginal flags. Every other Aboriginal property with an Aboriginal flag in the town was at risk of racially motivated vandalism and arson, but not the used-car yards.

That was a short, sharp lesson for me in the power of capitalism to cut through deeply embedded, intransigent race hatred. It was an epiphany: so, money did make the world go round, even in a situation where the money was in black hands. Yes, the spivs and dealers were exploiting Aboriginal people who lived in a world of poverty, but unlike anybody else in town, they turned up from down south and wanted to sell Aboriginal people something other than alcohol. I bought almost no clothes during the seven years that I lived in Alice Springs. The 'No Aborigines' rule extended to trying on clothes in shops. Getting service – and polite service at that – of any kind was just about impossible in Alice Springs a quarter of a century ago. But an Aboriginal person could buy a second-hand car or a vehicle-load of alcohol, no questions asked.

In fact, we could buy alcohol just about anywhere in Alice Springs. There were more licensed alcohol takeaway outlets per head of population than anywhere else in the country. We could buy it at supermarkets, at petrol stations, at the Elders rural supplies store, at sandwich shops, at pubs over the counter, and around the side at the 'animal bars', the counter at a hotel window reserved for serving 'blacks only'. Whites were served in the driveway section or at the front bar.

In the last lecture, I explained the transformation of the mining industry from the bare-knuckled approach of the 1960s through to the early 1990s, when access to Aboriginal land and reserves for mining projects involved the imposition of projects without consultation or negotiation, forced removals, and no regard for the impacts the projects had on

Aboriginal communities. But with the implementation of land rights and the recognition of native title, which required mining companies to negotiate with affected Aboriginal people, thousands of agreements acknowledging these impacts and providing benefits have changed the economic situation of Indigenous Australia irrevocably. Thousands of jobs, scores of contracting businesses and income streams from native title payments are the result, and would form the basis of an economic future if only government policy settings would move from protectionism to economic empowerment.

These developments did not come about without decades of rancorous debate and litigation by Aboriginal and Torres Strait Islander people, as I explained in the last lecture. The conflict between the mining industry and Aboriginal people occurred at the coincidence of the third mining boom in the late 1960s and early 1970s with the reforms of the 1970s, when land rights, civil rights and legislative rejection of racism brought Aboriginal people in from the cold.[1]

But there was another confluence of factors at the time that has had an enduring impact on Australian society, and explains much about the entrenched poverty in Aboriginal communities, despite the opportunities provided by the private sector: the legalisation of sales of alcohol to Aboriginal people, the emergence of the environmental movement, and the romanticisation of Aboriginal people as the 'new noble savages'. All occurred during the same period in Australia, the late 1960s and throughout the 1970s, and formed a toxic social and political brew. These became the most difficult of all the obstacles hindering Aboriginal economic development.

In the previous lecture, I referred to attitudes among the left, and among those opinion leaders who hang on to the idea of the 'new noble savage': how for them Aboriginal poverty is invisible, masked by their 'wilderness' ideology; how they describe the Aboriginal situation through a peculiarly racist lens – by means of extreme conservationist or 'wilderness' rhetoric. Whenever an Aboriginal group negotiates with a resource extraction company there is an unspoken expectation that no Aboriginal group should become engaged in any economic development. Most environmental campaigners, especially the members of the Wilderness Society, tolerate Aboriginal people as caretakers of wilderness only. They turn up at the gates of mining and gas projects, aligning themselves with a few disaffected Aboriginal people, to protest even when the majority of traditional owners have negotiated the settlement. This means, in practical terms, that they will only tolerate Aboriginal people living on their land if they live in horrific poverty and remain uneducated and isolated.

The extreme, entrenched poverty of such communities, deriving as it does from historical dispossession and economic exclusion, and, for the last forty years, high welfare dependency, gives a particular form to the kinds of consumption, distribution and marketing that take place in this distorted corner of the Australian economy. What the grog runners, spivs and drifters cunningly understand – more so than governments and banks – is the economic worth of these populations. So too do the large market players such as the supermarket chains, which hold a major position in the Aboriginal economy of the north, selling food at inflated prices and alcohol at low prices to Australia's poorest, sickest and most vulnerable people.

To understand how this came about, we need to go further back in history and trace the lineage of the 'new noble savage' from his ancestral roots. How did it happen that the economic life of Aboriginal people has come to mean mendicancy on the welfare state? How did it come to be that those of us who argue for jobs for Aboriginal people, for policies that encourage entrepreneurship among Aboriginal people, are despised and loathed by that section of the population that can only tolerate the 'cultural' Aborigine? Why does the left wing seem to hate the idea of a thriving, educated, economically engaged Aboriginal population?

The economic history of Aboriginal Australia – and there is one, and a fascinating one at that – has been shoved to the back of the stove. The deployment of a cultural analysis, an especially poor one, has been used to interpret Aboriginal life through texts as a series of theories with little attention to the downward-spiralling trends in health, employment, education and life expectancy in the Aboriginal population.

Aboriginal cultures are fascinating, and this may explain the reliance of analysts and academics on cultural explanations for the present situation. Too many ignore, and even fail to recognise, the role of economic history in producing the crippling disadvantages that hold so many Aboriginal people back, deprive them of the capacity to take up opportunities, and close the door on any possibility of a successful, healthy life.

How did the traditional economies collapse? In January 1788, Captain Arthur Phillip, a British navy officer, established a penal settlement, giving effect to Captain James Cook's declaration of possession (made on Possession Island off Cape York Peninsula in 1770), which applied to the eastern half of a still mysterious continent. What followed was Aboriginal subjugation, not only to a new polity but to a radically new economic regime. British graziers and farmers altered most Australian landscapes by clearing trees on a massive scale for their herds and crops. This, and the forced removal of populations by military, paramilitary and vigilante forces, as well as violence and disease epidemics, brought to an end the ancient hunting, gathering and fishing economy of the first Australians across most of the continent.

By the end of the 1940s, only a few Indigenous groups retained their pre-contact lifestyles and, although limited, impaired or controlled by various means, those societies continued in Cape York, Central Australia and the Western Desert, and also in some areas of the Top End of the Northern Territory and in the Kimberley region of Western Australia. The traditional economic systems had collapsed across much of the continent, even in Central Australia, and it became almost impossible to provide sufficient food by traditional means. The ration system[2] contributed to this collapse as much as dispossession, but without rations, and even with them, many Aboriginal people starved or suffered severe malnutrition. As a result, the Indigenous populations that survived became more entangled in the new economy that had supplanted their own. They were largely treated as indentured, controlled or unfree labour, and it is clear that a form of slavery existed in various places. In Queensland, such wages as were paid were confiscated by the state;[3] here the law requiring that equal wages be paid to Aboriginal workers only came into being in the 1980s. Even so, Indigenous people found livelihoods and became essential to the success of several industries, especially cattle production. From the hop growers of Corranderk to the pearl-shell divers of the Torres Strait, the ingenuity of the first Australians is as marvellous as their very survival in the dire conditions of frontier conflict.

The assimilation policies that were formalised and entrenched by state and territory governments of the 1940s meant that the role of Aboriginal labour fitted in with a caste system that operated throughout the British Empire. It had been imposed in India, Africa and elsewhere, and was used as the means of extracting labour cheaply. This system relegated people to categories such as servants, coolies, indentured labourers, controlled populations, among others. In Australia, though, there could be no special arrangements with local chiefs or ruling families, as had occurred under the Raj in India or with the ruling aristocracies in Malaysia and some African colonies.

As in most of the world's hunter-gatherer societies, leadership in Aboriginal Australia was situational. There were no chiefs or ruling hereditary elites that could press their populations into service for the plantations, slave trade and other economic ventures, as the comprador classes in British colonies elsewhere had done in order to maintain their power and privilege. These compradores – or native-born agents – served the colonisers and trading empires as collaborators in commercial transactions, a practice that did not take root in Australia because of the frontier violence to 'disperse' Aboriginal populations, especially through the campaigns of armed white-settler vigilante groups and the Native Mounted Police who were forced into service, and of the existence of slavery and controlled labour.

The terrible state of affairs that the colonial regime had brought about lingered for another sixty years, and as the living conditions grew worse for dispersed Aboriginal populations, denied rights as citizens and discriminated against at every turn, the problem became impossible to ignore.

The Australian frontier was a notably masculine one, and miscegenation with Aboriginal women was common. The embarrassment of coloured children became a critical issue when their origins posed a threat to the establishment of the British way of life in the colonies, as British wives were imported to establish household domesticity. This led to policies aimed at removing Aboriginal children from their families. While eugenicist in their motivation, these were also labour policies intended to supplement the servile population with trained children. Those exempted from these policies remained on Crown reserves, gazetted for the benefit of Aborigines, whose racial identity was, at least formally, that of 'full-bloods'. The reality on the ground was, of course, quite different; reserve populations remained mixed and the goal of racial hygiene and segregation was never achieved in practice, a fact that the idealists who hold to fantastic ideas about authentic traditional Aborigines should consider. The idea that a burgeoning coloured population in northern Australia was a security threat in the first half of the twentieth century showed how xenophobic the Anglo-Saxon majority was.

The social revolutions of the 1960s and 1970s, in which Gough Whitlam, Charles Perkins, H. C. 'Nugget' Coombs, W. E. H. Stanner, Barry Dexter and many others played key roles, could be described as a series of odd, distinctively Australian decolonisation experiments. In retrospect, it has become clearer that the isolation of remnant Indigenous populations in an archipelago of Crown reserves posed a series of economic and social policy conundrums. Only a small number of men, we can see now, had turned their minds to the human rights disaster located on the outskirts of many rural towns and in city ghettoes. Race and economy were intertwined throughout Australia's history, although this historical process was almost invisible in the cities.

Charles Rowley's trilogy, especially *The Destruction of Aboriginal Society*, published in 1970, the most detailed economic history of Australia's racial frontiers ever written, explains the history and facts of Aboriginal life on the margins of Australian society and economy up to the 1960s. Charles Rowley described the situation in the far-flung, small, dispersed Aboriginal groups living on Crown reserves as an Australian version of the USSR's notorious 'gulag archipelago'.

He had declined the invitation to join Stanner, Nugget Coombs and Barry Dexter on the Council for

Aboriginal Affairs. This august body advised several prime ministers, and its work represented a sharp break with the post-frontier thinking its members encountered in their discussions with politicians, officials, missionaries, reserve superintendents, and Aboriginal and Torres Strait Islander people throughout the continent. Rowley later took the post as head of the Aboriginal Land Fund Commission, a task more to his inclination, given his interest in economic matters.

What is most striking in Rowley's works are the origins of present-day debates, as they may be called, about Indigenous policy in Australia. It was clear to the members of the Council for Aboriginal Affairs that, for thousands of Aboriginal communities across the country and for the rapidly growing number of Aboriginal people who were already participating in the workforce (or wanted to), there was a storm of issues brewing.

This crisis of modernisation in what had been missions and post-frontier-administered settlements accelerated with the Equal Wages Case in 1968, two years after the Wave Hill strike led by Vincent Lingiari, and the upheaval that followed when thousands of Aboriginal pastoral workers were abruptly dismissed. While the case was fought on behalf of the pastoralists by wealthy absentee lessees who retained John Kerr (later Australia's governor-general) as counsel, many small operators probably could not have afforded to pay wages to Aboriginal workers. Legal counsel representing the Aboriginal workers successfully argued the Aboriginal equal wages case before the Arbitration Tribunal. The equal wages award was a pyrrhic victory, however. Some states had long before instituted 'training' wages for Aboriginal people and indentured domestic servitude for Aboriginal children, and there was little likelihood of Aboriginal people being paid equal wages by either the state governments or employers in the pastoral and agricultural industries where Aboriginal people had served as rural labour.

It became evident that modern land titles were required to enable Commonwealth investment in desperately needed infrastructure, and also to ensure the security of these communities from further incursions by corrupt or malign Aboriginal Affairs officials in the states and territories. The Commonwealth *Social Security Act* had been extended for the first time to particular Aboriginal Australians only in 1966.[4]

After the Amendments to the Constitution following the 1967 Referendum, the Council's members were faced with the question of whether to bring Aborigines residing on reserves in from the cold, or to leave them in the economic wilderness that the Aboriginal protectorates had created. Later, in 1972, Rowley became involved with the establishment of the Aboriginal Land Fund Commission. The commission purchased pastoral leases for resident or nearby Aboriginal groups that had been marginalised in the late 1960s by angry white pastoralists who refused to pay equal wages to their Aboriginal workers.

Later, when their stake in the industry dramatically increased, Aboriginal pastoralists found that, whereas these post-feudal holdings could support an owner-manager family, only agribusiness on a much vaster scale (or involving much more profitable uses of land, and diversification) could economically support communities of several hundred Aboriginal people. Meanwhile, in Australia's 'gulag archipelago', missionaries were asked to leave the reserves, and reserve superintendents were replaced by community councils. The missionaries and superintendents had managed the cattle herds, sawmills, bakeries, butcheries, small cropping projects and cottage industries in these small Aboriginal communities, and as they left, these industries and enterprises began to deteriorate slowly into a state of irreversible failure, or simply closed down overnight.

The order, discipline and management culture of the old imperial hands had been the glue that, however tenuously, held together the imposed regimes of settlement on the scattered Aboriginal groups in the hinterland. Years of apartheid in the education system and the almost total exclusion of Aboriginal people from normal training, apprenticeships and employment resulted in a rapidly growing Indigenous underclass in the towns and cities, as Aboriginal families fled from the reserves during the 1960s and 1970s to take advantage of the new wave of tolerance and progressive thinking.[5]

Then two new forces collided with the Aboriginal world. Just as it seemed that the social and economic issues affecting Aboriginal people might be understood by more compassionate voters – 96 per cent of them had voted 'yes' for Aboriginal rights in the 1967 National Referendum – the mining boom of the 1970s and the worldwide leftist civil rights and Indigenous movements precipitated a furious debate. Should Aboriginal reserves, freeholds and leases be readily accessed by mining companies without regard to the consequences for already impoverished and disadvantaged communities, or should there be a special category of rights for Indigenous people, especially those minorities encapsulated in settler states, where their fate was abuse and marginalisation?[6]

The Aboriginal movement for land rights established the battleground for political rights for the next three decades, and its impact was both beneficial – with the return of large areas of land to the rightful owners – and detrimental. Not until after the passage of the Commonwealth's *Native Title Act* in late 1993, a quarter of a century after the Referendum, were some of the more incendiary issues in this dispute, which had consumed three generations of Aboriginal leaders,[7] partially resolved.

Into the conflict came environmentalists and 'wilderness' campaigners, attaching themselves to dissident Aboriginal groups at Jabiluka in western Arnhem Land, in Cape York, and elsewhere, opposing development, not because of its impacts on Aboriginal people, but to preserve nature, biodiversity and the 'wilderness'. Whether Aboriginal groups had projects imposed on them or negotiated successful settlements, these professional protesters, supported by sophisticated non-government organisations that raised funds from a gullible public, accused Aboriginal leaders of 'selling out'. Not once have so-called 'green' groups campaigned against Aboriginal poverty. They simply assume that this is the normal state of affairs for the natives. They and the members of the Australian Labor Party (ALP) have taken the Aboriginal electorate for granted since the days of Gough Whitlam's reforming government.

Recently, this changed. First, Ken Wyatt ran for the Liberal Party in the seat of Hasluck in Western Australia and became the first Aboriginal person elected to the House of Representatives. Others had been elected to state and territory parliaments, and in the Northern Territory, the ALP took advantage of the large Aboriginal population and governed for eleven years from 2001 to 2012, with several elected Aboriginals serving in the Cabinet. In 2012, fed up with the failure of the Territory government to serve their interests fairly, the Aboriginal voters brought about a dramatic game change. Aboriginal voters in the bush threw out the government that had ignored them, delivering victory to the Country Liberal Party. This extraordinary outcome – a first in Australian history – challenged mainstream perceptions about the marginal power of the Aboriginal vote. The voter turnout across the Territory was an unusually high 76.9 per cent; three in ten Territorians are

Aboriginal. They were fed up with left-wing causes imposed from 'down south', be it live-cattle export restrictions, opposition to mining, or rolling back the intervention.

Once the party of the frontiersmen and spruikers, and rabidly opposed to Aboriginal rights, the Country Liberal Party has changed its colour – four of its members in the new Northern Territory assembly are outback Aboriginal leaders. It seems the Territory's rural conservatives have finally figured out that they have more in common with Aboriginal people than with their kin in the cities. Both groups need land-based industries to support their economies and way of life. Both share a deep disdain for greens, animal liberationists and bureaucrats, whether from Darwin or Canberra.

The Territory's Labor government had disbanded Aboriginal councils to create 'super shires'. This enraged Aboriginal people, especially the former council members and employees, in hundreds of townships and homeland communities, which were now managed from afar by white town clerks. State and territory governments have long used untied Commonwealth grants for 'Indigenous Affairs' as a general-purpose slush fund for everyone except the poorest of the poor, the remote Aboriginal populations.[8] In the same way, the vast sums committed to the intervention had been soaked up by the bureaucrats and consultants.

Perhaps the Northern Territory branch of the ALP thought it could get away with the usual game of spending the Commonwealth's Aboriginal dollars centrally, mostly in Darwin, and depriving the bush communities of their entitlements. This time they went too far. By disempowering the communities – shutting down their councils and, in effect, shutting them up – they betrayed them.

But the most significant factor was the Aboriginal body politic itself. Strong local leaders have worked hard to bring economic development to Indigenous communities where welfare has turned residents into perpetual mendicants begging from the state. Time and again, native title groups have spent years getting an agreement with a resource company over the line, negotiating income streams that might shift Indigenous people from the margins to the centre of regional economic development in return for land access, only for a ragtag team of 'wilderness' campaigners to turn up with an entourage of disaffected (and perpetually dissident) Aboriginal protesters to stop development at the eleventh hour.

The legacy of these developments is a clutch of phenomena that work to alienate Aboriginal people, to impoverish them, to under-develop them, to exclude them. The fight back is another long story, and in the next lecture, I will turn to those ideas that have inspired the economic renewal of Aboriginal Australia.

THREE

LEGACIES, NEW PARTNERSHIPS AND PLANS: HOW TRADITIONAL OWNERS CAN SETTLE THEIR GRIEVANCES WITH THE OLD MINING CULTURE

Ten years ago, I asked a young Aboriginal man working on a mine site if he enjoyed his job. He was on a team that worked a twelve-hour daily shift on a cycle of rosters that meant two weeks on the job, then one week off, and his home was about four hours' drive north of the mine. Confronted by a nosy older woman like me, he mumbled his answer, 'Yeah.'

'Why is that?' I asked.

'I'm out of the community for a couple of weeks and I don't have to put up with the fighting.'

I asked him if he had saved any money. He had bought a house, he said.

He and a number of other young Aboriginal men were training as members of a team that provided mechanical repair, among a variety of services, to other units in the operation. His blunt answers to my questions reverberated in my mind. I thought about the changes in his life that employment on this project must have wrought. It had given him some financial freedom, and freedom from the *Sturm und Drang* of community life, where interpersonal, inter-family and inter-clan conflict can sweep everyone up in a never-ending monsoon of suspicion, accusation, abuse and violence. Young men, as much as young women, are all too often the victims.

His matter-of-fact declaration of his hard-won ticket to freedom jolted me out of any sense of complacency about the benefits of jobs at the mine. The ripple effects were visible and important. Others at the mine saw the extraordinary changes in the lives of the young people who stepped into that world, and it motivated them to set bold targets for Aboriginal employment. The employment levels achieved at this site, the Argyle Diamond Mine, have not been met at all mine sites. There are reasons for this, and as will be explained in this lecture, the absence of corporate social responsibility and a long history of blatant injustice are two of them. Each case is different, however, and not all historical impacts are immutable.

The negotiations for the Argyle Diamond Mine Indigenous Land Use Agreement took place from about 2001 to 2004, and it was registered with the Native Title Tribunal in 2005. The project itself had started back in the late 1970s. For three decades, the company's engagement with the local Aboriginal people was founded on a flawed and profoundly unjust Good Neighbour Agreement, as it was called. At best, this was implemented with benign incompetence; at worst, it denied the traditional owners and neighbouring communities any semblance of fair treatment in employment opportunities, and, for much of that period, there was little respect for their culture and sacred sites. This approach began to change in 1995 when Leon Davis, then Chief Executive Officer of CRA Ltd (which soon became Rio Tinto Ltd), made a headland speech that shifted the industry's paradigm. The paradigm had till then been led by Hugh Morgan's Western Mining Corporation which then held sway in the main industry association, the Australian Mining Industry Association (AMIC). The Association funded and designed several divisive television and print media campaigns depicting Aboriginal desires as childish, illegitimate and shamelessly based in an anti-Australian rent-seeking greed. Davis's acceptance of native title and move towards respect for traditional owners enraged Morgan and other industry leaders, but led to the sophistication in agreement-making that we witness today.[1] As with the Argyle Diamond Mine and Comalco cases, there were other legacy projects that required native title negotiations in order to expand operations by acquiring new lease areas.[2] In the case of the Argyle and the Comalco bauxite negotiations, apologies were given to the traditional owners by Brendan Hammond at Argyle, and by Premier Peter Beattie in 2001 in the case of Comalco, also acquired by Rio Tinto Ltd and later transferred to its subsidiary, Rio Tinto Alcan.[3] These apologies proved to be critical, not least because the traditional owners felt vindicated by the acknowledgement of the injustices, but also because they set the benchmark for relationships in the future.

While the clans affected by the activities of mining in the Kimberley and Cape York regions received acknowledgement of the damage done to them and their lands, others did not. The Gumatj and Rirratjingu clans of the Yolngu people of northeast Arnhem Land in the Northern Territory are also owed an apology, I believe, for the imposition of a bauxite mine on their land, but as far as I know none has been forthcoming. In 1973, Nabalco, a Swiss–Australian consortium, started mining and processing a 250-million tonne bauxite deposit (one of the world's largest), and established the new town of Gove, later called Nhulunbuy. Whereas until then the only incursions into this vast Aboriginal homeland had been the Methodist mission at Yirrkala, Dhupuma College, and some infrastructure dating from World War II, now there were a thousand white men building the refinery, port, mine infrastructure, town – and the longest conveyer belt in Australian history.

In an attempt to head off the incursion, the clan leaders drafted a petition on bark to the federal Parliament in Canberra, pleading that the mine should not proceed. The petition, now called the Bark Petition, was expressed in English and Yolngu Matha, and was painted with sacred designs. It was the first and, as far as I know, only petition to Parliament in an Aboriginal language. Galarrwuy Yunupingu was the interpreter for the elders who painted and wrote the Bark Petition, and also later in the Supreme Court proceedings in the famous Gove Case, which I will discuss briefly later. In 2007, Galarrwuy Yunupingu explained to an audience in Melbourne his own history in relation to the Barunga Statement, a similar painted petition, presented to Prime Minister Robert J. Hawke in 1988:

In 1988, with the late Arrernte leader Wenten Rubuntja, I led the Aboriginal people of the Northern Territory to make another bark petition, which is called the Barunga Statement. I presented it to the then Prime Minister Bob Hawke, who understood our reasoning. He wanted a treaty with us, but he was opposed in Canberra by both sides of politics.

At one point a few years ago I was so frustrated that I wanted to go and bring home the Barunga Statement from where it hung in Parliament.

It was prepared after great consultation with the traditional owners of the Northern Territory. It calls for Aboriginal self-management, a national system of land rights, compensation for loss of lands, respect for Aboriginal identity, an end to discrimination, and the granting of full civil, economic, social and cultural rights.

I am pleased that the Barunga Statement still hangs in Parliament.

But I had come to feel that its words had been
so ignored that the best thing to do would be to get
it out of the Parliament and take it home and bury
it in a bark coffin.

My cousin, Wali Wunungmurra, who is the
last living signatory to the original Bark Petition
told me recently that he wished to go and get that
petition, and take it home also.

These are the frustrations that men like Wali
and I live with.[4]

Galarrwuy was as frustrated with the mean response
to this later Barunga Statement, as his elders had been
with the silence to the original Bark Petition. In the
late 1960s, there had been an inquiry into the views
of the residents of Yirrkala, but to no avail. In 1971,
the Yolngu people decided to litigate. They asserted
their continuing ownership of traditional lands
by challenging the validity of the Commonwealth
government's grant of mining leases over their territory.
They brought the question of Aboriginal rights to land
and the concept of native title before the courts for the
first time in Australian history. The plaintiffs 'asserted
on behalf of the native clans they represented that those
clans and no others had in their several ways occupied

the areas from time immemorial as of right'. Their case, *Milirrpum v Nabalco Pty Ltd and the Commonwealth*[5] – or the Gove Land Rights Case – was, in the end, unsuccessful. The cast of characters included Mr Justice Blackburn presiding; legal counsel for the Yolngu plaintiffs, Mr Justice Woodward; anthropologists W. E. H. Stanner and R. M. Berndt presenting expert evidence; and Galarrwuy Yunupingu (later Chairman of the Northern Land Council) as interpreter for the Yolngu witnesses. Justice Blackburn found that native title was incapable of being recognised at common law in Australia.

Indeed, Justice Blackburn found that, 'If ever a system could be called "a government of laws, and not of men", it is that shown in the evidence before me'.[6] He found, however, that this system of laws was not one that the court could recognise.

He upheld the decisions of previous courts that the Crown was the source of all title to land, maintaining the status of Australia under the doctrine of *terra nullius*, and concluded that Indigenous interests in land had not survived the acquisition of sovereignty and did not form any part of the law of Australia. The decision was made despite the fact that many other common law jurisdictions, particularly Canada and the United States, had in various ways recognised the existence of Indigenous rights and interests.[7] It was this decision that was overthrown by the Mabo No. 2 case in the High Court of Australia in 1992, and which informed the *Native Title Act.*

The decision was a tragedy, just as much a tragedy as the destruction of landscapes and sacred sites that followed, because it denigrated Yolngu laws and traditions.

The insult has never been forgotten.

The existence of the bauxite mine and its voracious culture on the lands of these clans poisoned relations between the Aboriginal people and each successive company that has owned it. The Yolngu people were marginalised in their own country. The impact of twentieth-century Australian mining culture went below the surface and in the 1960s caused anguish to the Yolngu men and women who witnessed violent changes to their landscapes, beaches, waters and, ultimately, their lifestyles. The parents of that period were shocked when many of their children became debilitated by alcohol, drugs, unemployment and a new phenomenon – poverty. The elders rued the injustice and the impacts, especially the psychological impacts, with a growing sense of frustration and alienation, as each succeeding company that owned the mine refused to negotiate with them.

This changed in 2007 when Rio Tinto Ltd acquired the Canadian company Alcan, which itself had acquired the mine from Nabalco in 2002. The Rio Tinto Alcan agreement, or Gove Mining Agreement, was signed on 13 May 2011.

The agreement with Rio Tinto Alcan encompasses outstanding long-term financial terms and opportunities to tap into the regional economy created by the mine. Now operated by Pacific Aluminium, the downturn in bauxite prices globally has engendered caution in the parties and also a sense of urgency. The Yolngu at last have an agreement governing the operation, which gives them an economic stake in the region. So no opportunity can be lost in this precarious situation.

Since 1998, this clan has welcomed thousands of visitors to the annual Garma Festival of Traditional Culture, and engaged leaders from around Australia and the globe with their traditional hospitality and robust religious life. More than their cultural wealth has grown with each festival. The clan leaders have been developing an economic strategy for some years, assisted by legal firms committed to Aboriginal people. They are transforming their traditional economy, culture and ceremonial life with the leverage that strong land rights has provided. They are reinstating the work ethic that underpinned their ancient and resilient society, and building a diversified regional economy to free their members from the drudgery of poverty and the indignity of welfare dependence.

Like their compatriots in Western Australia, the Yolngu have also turned to the resource industry as a springboard for business development. In 2007, the Gumatj clan established and became majority owners in a mining and exploration company, Dhupuma Resources Pty Ltd, and other corporations that conduct commercial and social enterprises. In 2012, at the Garma Festival, Gumatj executives signed an agreement with Geodynamics Pty Ltd with the goal of establishing a geothermal project on Gumatj land to provide a much-needed source of energy for local industry. With their own corporations operating, they are developing mining and other ventures on their own land.

Yet despite this drive to engage working-age people in the workforce, very few Yolngu people work for the mine. Only a handful have ever worked there in the more than forty years of its operation, and this refusal, I believe, is attributable to the sadness, grief and anger of the elders whose world changed with a sharp shock, leaving them with an affective burden that has been passed down the generations, along with all the cultural wealth they have to offer.

Galarrwuy Yunupingu, whose presence throughout this history has been decisive, is like many of our generation: old school in his attitudes and habits. He is disciplined and stern. He has borne the mantle of conferred leadership, in clan and ceremonial matters, across a vast area, and during his years as Chair of the Northern Land Council, with dignity and perseverance, taking his responsibilities seriously and working diligently. In a series of speeches, he has rejected the protectionist, welfarist approach in Aboriginal policy and demanded a sensible approach to economic development, and parity in education and employment.

The solution he devised to combat the discrimination by the white workers that excluded and alienated two generations of Yolngu from employment at the mine was to create Yolngu enterprises to create jobs. There are currently forty men and women employed in clan projects who would not otherwise be in work. One project involves harvesting the timber removed from the mine site and elsewhere, and operating mobile sawmills to produce timber for the construction of houses, buildings and fine handcrafted furniture. These projects have been developed with assistance from Forestry Tasmania.

Also, under the terms of the agreement, they are guaranteed rights to use the mine's batch plant concrete casting moulds for the production of concrete, as well as the Old Brickworks, and will purchase aggregate and cement at cost price. They also have the rights to scrap metal and construction steel for the purpose of house construction.

Gumatj also negotiated a preferential right to the waste management of the mine site and intend to establish a long-term agreement.

The opposition of green or environmental campaign groups to the timber business was a slap in the face for the Yolngu, who for more than a quarter of a century have run the most successful biodiversity and environmental conservation program through their Dhimurru Aboriginal Corporation. The media in Darwin covered with gusto the ludicrous complaints and assertions from the green campaigners, and vilified Galarrwuy Yunupingu in an appalling way. This was a return to the Jabiluka Camp tactics that involved years of protest at the Jabiluka uranium mine, bitterness and little result in western Arnhem Land.[8] But Galarrwuy's steady approach won out, and all the claims against him and the Gumatj clan were proved wrong.

The Gumatj projects are an example of diversification and coexistence: custom and cultural traditions of kinship are accommodated in their workplaces, with cousins working together and teams harmonised by having men and women in the correct customary relationships. They enter the Gumatj workforce without sacrificing their cultural selves. The obligation to attend ceremonies is no longer an excuse not to work, and the leaders, while not always heeded, demand a full workday. During times of ceremonies, workers start early in the morning, continue until three o'clock in the afternoon, and arrive at the ceremony at four o'clock when the *yidaki*, or didgeridoo, announces its commencement.

The success of this model lies in the affirmation by leaders of their commitment to land, culture and ceremony, but also to a work ethic and economic drive; all these values coexist and strengthen the group. This renewal has come after forty years of disappointment, anger and frustration. Galarrwuy and his fellow clan leaders have finally seized control of their destiny with a powerful vision of the future. Some might call this self-determination, but I have witnessed these leaders grow in intellectual understanding of their predicament, in their determination to solve problems, and in their desire to be their own agents, to join with committed people offering their expertise to develop new institutions and cultural innovations. The change has been radical but incremental, as with each success, more challenges arise to be faced.

With the establishment of a new school at Gunyangara for their children in 2012, they are rapidly realising their vision. Yet there is much more to be done in educating Yolngu youth. 'Work readiness' is an industry term used to describe the necessary skills for employment: literacy and numeracy, a driver's licence, safety training, and discipline. Galarrwuy Yunupingu, like all those people involved in the challenge of Aboriginal economic development, understands that education is the key. In 2007 he said, 'These children must have a future, which means economic development.' His focus is developing an education institution for the youth and adults of the region to give them the capabilities to make choices about their futures.

This bauxite mine in northeast Arnhem Land, the bauxite mine in western Cape York, and the Argyle

Diamond Mine in the Kimberley region are referred to as 'legacy' projects. The meaning is a technical and legal one. The projects required native title agreements to expand their operations or to renew leases. Their social and historical legacy before the advent of Aboriginal rights was a disgrace, and a long list of grievances – discrimination, unemployment, poverty, and exclusion from decisions about cultural and environmental impacts – were required to be addressed when native title rights finally enabled the traditional owners to bargain for a better deal. The native title agreements have achieved a measure of justice, and importantly, economic justice.

In a Mabo Day address in 2005, the Minister for Indigenous Affairs, the Hon. Jenny Macklin, raised the issue of converting mining agreement payments to public funds to close the gap. A taxation regime to achieve this was eventually outlined in a white paper, or ministerial discussion paper. Only in 2012, after years of lobbying, did the Commonwealth concede that these funds were not assessable for taxation purposes until they were distributed to native title holders. For almost five years, the taxation issues have been in question, making it difficult for many groups to plan and implement their strategies with any sense of security.

As we have seen, some native title groups have developed innovative schemes for investing the financial benefits of their agreements with mining companies in long-term community and economic development. The poorest people in Australia, the first peoples, from whom all hereditary assets – land, waters, even stone tools – were confiscated, are investing the first payments in lieu of compensation in an economic future. Meanwhile, government policies and programs have rarely been helpful in these situations. Only corporations and philanthropic bodies offer sensible financial and economic advice to these groups to give them the knowledge to operate in the market system effectively. These developments are in their infancy.

The native title regime has reached the crossroads where the 'market' and 'non-market' pathways of human social development have intersected. The negotiating sector of the native title system arrived at this junction some time ago, while governments and sections of the native title industry are trailing behind the negotiators and a few canny lawyers from private firms and some native title representative bodies working with the traditional owners.

So what economic development policies work in this arena?

Mining companies pay financial benefits in these settlements in lieu of the Crown obligation to compensate for extinguishment of native title. Because state governments have rarely honoured this constitutional and legal obligation, companies bear the cost. Why isn't there a 100 per cent exemption for all the costs of negotiated settlements with Aboriginal people, or the costs of Aboriginal employment and training in the mining industry, or the establishment of viable Aboriginal institutions to govern these arrangements? Instead of incentives to assist in this enterprise, there remain obstacles and disincentives in tax policy and practice, and in corporate law and governance for this highly specialised area of Aboriginal development.

Taxation income ought to be allocated to the very regions and communal lands where the wealth was generated. Yet even though this would be the most intelligent policy response for a number of reasons, and would accelerate Aboriginal employment, it would not by itself solve the fundamental problem.

In developing countries, natural resource accounts – a good example is the one established by the Timor Leste government – are regarded as best practice. They are designed to avoid 'resource curse' impacts and to secure a proportion of the profits from extracting mineral resources to enhance living standards and secure a worthwhile lifestyle for future generations. This is indeed one of the principal purposes of the Aboriginal trusts that receive native title payments. While the transaction costs remain high, the flow of payments will be reduced or nullified if the projects are unsustainable. Some, including the Nhulunbuy mine, are marginal because of commodity prices, debt structures, rising costs of labour, and other factors.

The latest reforms proposed for the not-for-profit sector, including charities, trusts and some of the entities typically operating in the Aboriginal domain, may be important. But the constant shadow of doubt over the policy and legislative arrangements in this area place already fragile Aboriginal governance and management initiatives in difficulty. Governments experiment far too much in the Aboriginal world. The change is constant and unsettling. A simple saying is appropriate here: less is more. And while attempts are made to be less opaque, there is room for improvement in the involvement of Aboriginal people in the development of policies and laws.

Taxation incentives and a reduction in the extraordinary government regulation and surveillance of Aboriginal endeavours urgently require reform. The ability of small, often geographically remote Aboriginal groups to innovate and diversify, as the Yolngu have, is in jeopardy while governments and their agencies are sluggish, traditional and heavy-handed in their responses. How can these critical matters be improved? In the final lecture, I will address some of these issues.

FOUR

THE FIRST AUSTRALIANS' GIFT TO THE WORLD: 30 MILLION HECTARES OF PROTECTED AREAS TO CONSERVE ENVIRONMENTS AND BIODIVERSITY

I had been searching for the quintessential statement by a 'wilderness' campaigner in opposition to Aboriginal interests to illustrate the problem I referred to in earlier lectures: the refusal among the romantics, leftists and worshippers of nature to admit that Aboriginal people, like other humans, have an economic life, are caught up in the transforming encounter with modernity, and have economic rights. A succinct and illuminating quote was not difficult to find. Then I came across something more disturbing than the usual from poorly informed zealots. When respected scientists engage in public debate and castigate Aboriginal rights, a different order of offence is caused. Like many Australians, I respect the work of Tim Flannery as an advocate for environmental conservation. I have disagreed with him publicly twice. My first disagreement with him in 1994 concerned his speculation that the first Australians, some thousands of years ago, were responsible for the extinction of the Australian megafauna. Several scientists have dismissed his claim, as did I, as I have explained in the Introduction to these lectures.[1] His highly speculative theory has been damaging to Aboriginal people, particularly because it has become the 'respectable' source for hateful claims made by racists in the 'green' movement, advocates for Indigenous genocide, and grazier activists intent on turning back Aboriginal rights. Then, while I was writing this lecture, Tim Flannery's *Quarterly Essay: After the future, Australia's new extinction crisis,* was published.

He writes in that essay:

… mining often takes priority over nature protection. Even under Labor governments with a strong green bent, *national parks are not always*

safe [my emphasis]. In 2010, the Queensland Bligh
government began the process of de-gazetting a
large part of Mungkan Kaanju National Park on
Cape York Peninsula, with a view to giving the
land back to its traditional Aboriginal owners.[2]

What is wrong with Flannery's idea that the land is not
'safe' if it is owned by an Aboriginal person or entity?
Flannery has publicly denied this interpretation of
his essay[3], but I find it difficult to ignore the potential
implication (which, as I say, was not his intention)
that this statement asserts national park status (which
is not a guarantee of conservation in Queensland
where national parks in Cape York are licensed for
cattle grazing) is superior to Aboriginal ownership.
By itself, the objection to Aboriginal ownership, if it
were read that way, would be offensive. The statement
could imply that such a title is less 'safe' from mining
than if it remains national park. In my view it also
has the potential to imply that any title owned by a
non-Aboriginal person is 'safer' than one owned by
an Aboriginal person or entity. Neither is the case. In
Australian law the Crown not only has the power to
de-gazette national parks but to acquire compulsorily
any land title for any purpose. Our Constitution

requires that landowners be compensated at fair market value for such acquisitions. (As an aside, I note that, in relation to compulsory acquisition of native title, Australian governments have usually ignored this constitutional responsibility.) Thus, it makes no difference at law if the title is a national park, freehold, pastoral lease or any other title. As well, it makes no difference if the titleholder is white or Aboriginal, or any other nationality for that matter. Only the Crown, or in this case, the Queensland government, gives approval for mining projects.

I reiterate: faced with a mining project, Aboriginal landowners in Australia are in the same position as all other landowners, apart from the very limited circumstances in the Northern Territory. The *Native Title Act* provides only a 'Right to Negotiate', but in Queensland, the Native Title Tribunal decisions have conspired to deny native title parties even effective use of those rights by a legal sleight of hand.

I am not suggesting that Flannery is merely a 'wilderness' campaigner, and acknowledge his contribution to science in the field of palaeontology. Yet, the excerpt from his essay offended me and several Aboriginal leaders who corresponded with me on this matter. I could assume that Flannery knows nothing about the history of this national park, and attribute his remark to simple ignorance. However, that would be an insult to his intelligence. This national park area was purchased by the Aboriginal Land Fund and the Aboriginal traditional owners in 1976, when it was the Archer River Pastoral Holding, a pastoral lease. The refusal of the Bjelke-Petersen government to transfer the title to Aboriginal people was the subject of one of the most extraordinary High Court cases in Australian history, *Koowarta v. Bjelke-Petersen* (1982). The lease area was immediately gazetted as a national park by the Queensland government, and such gazettals became a standard tactic to prevent Aboriginal purchases of land. Premier Bligh returned the area to the traditional owners because of the blatant racism involved in the decision by the Queensland Cabinet in 1976 to disallow any Aboriginal land ownership by Aboriginal people on the grounds of race. By overcoming in this way the historical legacy of racism that she had inherited, Bligh was able to deflect criticism of her performance with respect to the Wild Rivers legislation and gazettals of Aboriginal-owned land under that Act to prevent any developments and improvements.

An example of the implications of Flannery's remark can be seen in the gazettal of large areas of

Aboriginal-owned land in Cape York Peninsula by the Bligh government under the *Wild Rivers Act 2005*. The opposition to the legislation by Aboriginal landowners to several gazetted areas was completely ignored by the Queensland government under Premier Anna Bligh. The racist assumption of the proponents of the *Wild Rivers Act*, particularly the Wilderness Society leaders who negotiated the legislation with her government, was that the rivers were 'unsafe' from development while the banks and river basins were owned by Aboriginal people. What were the traditional owners going to do to these rivers? Frighten the fish? This is not a trivial remark. The idea of Aboriginal people as fundamentally polluting is an old racist idea, and explains why our ancestors were incarcerated in reserves and stripped of property and freedom.

If Indigenous people in Australia had a full, domestic legal right to the United Nations principle of free, prior and informed consent, the situation would be different in relation to mining. But this is not the case. As I have described in previous lectures, Aboriginal groups have struggled with the injustice of mining for fifty years, and have had to carve out a niche for their own survival in the midst of careless, racist disregard for their wellbeing.

For forty years, this racist assumption in the green movement about Aboriginal people being the enemies of the wilderness has been a leitmotif in deals between conservation groups and state governments to deny Aboriginal people their rights as landowners and citizens of Australia. The *Wild Rivers Act*, now repealed by the Newman government, was one of many deals of this kind.

There is another issue to consider in this presumption that we Aboriginal people are the threat to nature. Most Australians, until recently, were spared the experience of living with mining projects. With the development of shale gas and fracking projects and their expansion into valuable farming land, farmers, rural-and even suburban-dwelling Australians have objected stridently, and begun to demand protections much as Aboriginal people did fifty years ago when large-scale mining projects impacted on their world. Most mining projects are located in remote and rural Australia; 60 per cent of them are located near Aboriginal communities. It is Aboriginal people who have borne the brunt of the direct impacts of mining and, as I explained in earlier lectures, tamed the industry with a range of campaigns and strategies during the last half century.

Moreover, Aboriginal land is targeted both by mining companies and conservation campaigners precisely because it is Aboriginal land.[4] The presumption by conservationists that these areas need to be rescued from Aboriginal people – as made clear by Tim Flannery and in the Wild Rivers saga in Queensland – is a strange twist on the racist fiction of *terra nullius* overturned by the Mabo case. They are not wilderness areas. They are Aboriginal homelands, shaped over millennia by Aboriginal people. Our customary and traditional governance systems exist, and continue as rational systems of law in the lives of thousands of Aboriginal people. These vast areas owned by Aboriginal people are the repository of Australia's mega diversity of fauna, flora and ecosystems not only because of the ancient Aboriginal system of management, but because Aboriginal people fought to protect their territories from white incursion. While it is a miracle that they have survived colonisation and white settlement, the real wonder is the capacity for innovation and ingenuity that Aboriginal tradition allows. This is something that goes entirely unnoticed among conservation campaigners, and as we have seen, even among the intellectuals of the movement like Tim Flannery.

Some conservationists and conservation groups have been complicit in political chicanery, racism and further expropriation of our homelands, and for thirty years have been opposed to Aboriginal advancement. The examples are numerous, but time permits discussion of only one, a very pertinent one given Flannery's statement rebuking the return of the Mungkan Kaanju National Park on Cape York: the events leading up to the High Court case *Koowarta v. Bjelke-Petersen* in 1982.

From the early 1970s to the 1990s, Queensland state governments used environmental conservation legislation and instruments to prevent Aboriginal groups from acquiring and using land.[5] The most notorious of such actions was that taken against the late John Koowarta of the Winychanam group of Cape York, a sometime resident at Aurukun and also at settlements further inland. In February 1976, Koowarta and the Aboriginal Land Commission entered into a written contract with the lessees for the purchase of the Archer River Pastoral Holding lease, which was located on his traditional territory in central Cape York, and cattle and horses on the lease. The sale and transfer of the lease was subject to the approval or permission of the Minister for Lands of the State of

Queensland, Ken Tomkins, and, on 23 March 1976, the commission sought the consent of the minister to transfer the lease to the commission. Tomkins refused.[6] Queensland government policy explicitly opposed 'proposals to acquire large areas of additional freehold land or leasehold land for development by Aborigines or Aboriginal groups in isolation'.[7] The government instead gazetted a number of national parks over the pastoral properties that Aboriginal peoples had expressed interest in buying, in order to prevent them from legally purchasing the land.

On or about 8 December 1976, Minister Tomkins provided the reason for refusing to grant approval or permission to such transfer. His statement contained the following passage:

> The question of the proposed acquisition of
> Archer River Pastoral Holding comes within the
> ambit of declared Government policy expressed
> in [the] Cabinet decision of September 1972,
> which stated: 'The Queensland Government does
> not view favourably proposals to acquire large
> areas of additional freehold or leasehold land
> for development by Aborigines or Aboriginal
> groups in isolation.' In the light of this policy

the recent development whereby the Aboriginal Land Fund Commission sought to acquire by transfer Archer River Pastoral Holding was reported in detail to State Cabinet, whereupon Cabinet said in June 1976: '(1) That Cabinet's policy regarding Aboriginal reserve lands, as approved in Decision No. 17541 of 4 September 1972, remains unchanged. (2) That in accordance with such policy and as it is considered that sufficient land in Queensland is already reserved and available for use and benefit of Aborigines, no consent be given to the transfer of Archer River Pastoral Holding No. 4785 to the Aboriginal Land Fund Commission.'[8]

Koowarta's appeal to the High Court was successful. In 1982, the High Court overruled the Queensland government's action. Koowarta's case concerned the validity of certain sections of the *Racial Discrimination Act*, which had been challenged by the Queensland government. It was alleged that the Queensland government had breached the act by refusing to grant a lease to the Aboriginal Land Fund Commission. The court held that the legislation was valid as an exercise by the Commonwealth of the external affairs power.[9]

Despite their win in this case, Koowarta and the Winychanam group were never able to acquire title to their beloved country. The Queensland government had already gazetted the lease area as the Archer Bend National Park before the High Court handed down its decision.

I remind the reader that this national park is the same one that became the Mungkan Kaanju National Park; the same one which, because it was returned to its traditional owners, caused Tim Flannery to moan that national park status does not guarantee safety from Aboriginal ownership and to imply that it had fallen into the wrong hands. I should note that its correct name is Oyala Thumotan and the traditional owners have changed the name of the national park accordingly. How fitting that Flannery should insult the traditional owners and the memory of Koowarta, on behalf of the conservation movement in 2012, on the thirtieth anniversary of the Koowarta case and the twentieth anniversary of the Mabo case.

Although he was unable to acquire land because of the racist intransigence of Bjelke-Petersen's government, Koowarta nevertheless scored a key victory in opposing racial discrimination. The case also confirmed the role of the Commonwealth government in Aboriginal land rights legislation. The Koowarta case is the first example of the Commonwealth using the external affairs power as the basis for legislation able to limit the actions of state governments.

Even given the history of racist chicanery – such as the Koowarta case – and the deals with governments made by conservationists to colonise Aboriginal land under the green flag such as the *Wild Rivers Act* – the plain fact is that, far more than any other group of citizens in Australia, Aboriginal people have dedicated their land to environmental and biodiversity conservation. The facts prove Flannery and his colleagues in the so-called 'wilderness' movement wrong.

So far, under the Indigenous Protected Area scheme and other arrangements, Aboriginal people have dedicated more than 30 million hectares of their own land to environmental and biodiversity conservation. This represents more than 25 per cent of the National Reserve System, while Aboriginal people represent less than three per cent of the population.

Like indigenous peoples elsewhere, Aboriginal and Torres Strait Islander peoples of Australia are concerned to promote and maintain their active involvement in the pursuit of environmental security and sustainable economic livelihoods on their ancestral lands.

There are various legal and practical reasons for the Australian government to incorporate Indigenous customary interests into the broader Australian project of land, sea and resource conservation. Land and water subject to Indigenous ownership and governance constitutes a significant and substantial proportion – more than 20 per cent – of the Australian continent.[10]

Since the High Court's finding in the Mabo judgement[11] and the codification of the *Native Title Act 1993*, native title rights to land, sea and resources are now recognised in Australia's legislative landscape.[12] In 1999, some customary rights in fauna were also found to exist as a form of native title by the High Court of Australia.[13] Furthermore, Indigenous ownership and input to management of land will increase.[14]

Despite the influence of the North American model on the development of its national parks, Australia has taken a lead role in the development of joint management agreements with Indigenous groups in a few national parks. Nevertheless, in jointly managed parks where Indigenous people maintain ownership and various degrees of control over their estates, tensions still arise between western and Indigenous ways of practising land management. This is the case in the Kakadu and Uluru–Kata Tjuta National Parks, which are jointly managed by lease agreements between traditional Aboriginal landowners and the federal government.[15]

The Indigenous Protected Area program (IPA) was established in 1996 as a part of the federal government's intention to establish a National Reserve System and under pressure from Indigenous people to ensure that their wishes in relation to conservation were recognised.[16] The aim of the National Reserve Strategy was to 'establish and manage a comprehensive, adequate and representative system of protected areas covering Australia's biological diversity'.[17]

It aimed to address gaps in the kinds of ecosystems under protected area management, and divided the continent in eighty-five regions under a process called the Interim Biogeographic Regionalisation of Australia, based on factors associated with climate, lithology, geology, landforms and vegetation. This scheme provides the bioregional planning framework for developing the National Reserve System and is used to inform future land acquisitions. The usual method of adding to the nation's conservation estate is through the government purchase of land for dedication as parks and reserves.

However, as this planning framework was being drawn up, government officials noticed that, in some instances, Aboriginal people owned whole bioregions.

Moreover, the recently enacted native title law and the future act regime in the *Native Title Act 1993* were new and challenging issues that would impinge upon the government's appropriation of land for the National Reserve System. As well, the Indigenous Land Corporation, a statutory body set up to meet the needs of Indigenous groups unlikely to achieve success with native title claims, was likely to increase the size of the Indigenous estate through sizeable land purchases.

At the same time Indigenous landholders aspired to re-establish their land management traditions and cooperate with government conservation agencies and scientists to achieve these aspirations. They had initiated some projects and were planning more.[18]

These initiatives were complemented at the international level by a new system of protected area categories declared by the International Union for Conservation of Nature (IUCN), which substantially recognised the rights and interests of Indigenous people to own, manage and sustainably use areas of land and sea of high conservation value.[19]

These new categories allowed for the establishment of protected areas that linked land and associated cultural values managed through legal or other effective means. This created possibilities to enable Indigenous landowners to manage protected areas on parity with the mainstream protected area estate. These combined initiatives resulted in the federal conservation agency conducting a consultation process with Indigenous organisations and state conservation agencies to discuss the establishment of what would become the Indigenous Protected Area (IPA) program.[20]

Before the program commenced in 1996, however, Indigenous groups and their representative bodies came together at two national workshops and expressed interest in the IPA idea as it could be applied to land owned by Indigenous peoples, and made it clear that their consent was dependent on a number of conditions:

- That there would no loss of control over land by Indigenous people. (There was concern that government would try to take over the management of IPA land.)
- That landowners would make the decisions and the plan of management on their own terms.
- That the role of government would remain one of a 'good neighbour' providing advice and technical support on a needs basis on matters relating to issues such as weeds, feral animal management, and tourism infrastructure.

- That the commitment by government for the IPA program would be long term.
- That the government would address, as an issue of equity, Aboriginal involvement in protected area management for those groups that had no land base as a result of dispossession.[21]

Following these negotiations the federal government proceeded with the establishment of the program with two components: first, the development and declaration of Indigenous Protected Areas on Indigenous-owned land where land owners manage the land as independent bodies; and second, a program to assist and support Indigenous people to negotiate with state agencies land management roles in existing government-owned national parks and reserves through some type of co-management arrangement.

The program began in 1996 with an undertaking to develop twelve pilot projects in diverse locations including high-density settled areas and remote areas.

The first declared IPA was Nantawarrina near the Flinders Ranges in South Australia in August 1998.

By 2005 a further eighteen Indigenous Protected Areas had been declared, eleven others had been funded to pursue co-management arrangements in government-owned protected areas, and fourteen more groups received interim funding to investigate the possibility of establishing more such areas.

Since then, the scheme has expanded considerably. There are now fifty-one declared Indigenous Protected Areas in Australia covering, as I said, 30 million hectares and making up 25 per cent of the National Reserve System.

In addition, there are forty consultation projects across Australia and there are plans to expand the IPA area by 40 per cent over the next five years.[22]

Each Indigenous Protected Area has a plan of management, is declared under one or more IUCN categories, undergoes a process of public declaration, and is entirely managed by Indigenous landowners. Indigenous Protected Areas, such as Nantawarrina in South Australia and Deen Maar in southwest Victoria, once denuded farm and pastoral lands, are now significantly regenerated, prompting the return of a diversity of native species of flora and fauna.[23]

Indigenous Protected Area agreements are voluntary and are made between the policy and coordination section of the federal Department of Sustainability, and Indigenous communities, land councils and other Indigenous bodies. The security and viability of the scheme lies in the establishment of long-term land-use agreements offering financial support from the government. These take the form of contractual one-year Financial Assistance Agreements.[24]

With training and assistance, the Indigenous Protected Area programs have had the effect of empowering communities and providing significant environmental, economic, social and cultural benefits. Land management activities range from tourism management and visitor interpretative services to weed and feral animal management and land rehabilitation.

Indigenous land owners participating in the program have also begun entering conservation agreements with state conservation agencies, which provide them with additional technical advice, training capacity and access to powers relating to permits and law enforcement on their land. They are also building relationships with other state natural resource management agencies and non-government organisations, establishing partnerships and participating in joint projects and other activities that attract additional funding and expand the capacities of land owners to pursue their land management objectives. In some cases Indigenous groups are creating arrangements where other bodies, such mining and tourism companies, with interests in the region contribute funds to enable the management of Indigenous Protected Areas and surrounding Indigenous lands.

There are several extraordinary developments in Aboriginal participation in the 'green economy' that have resulted from innovative thinking in the Aboriginal world about sustainable development and preserving the environments in which Aboriginal society has survived for more than 50,000 years. Carbon farming, in particular, is popular with Aboriginal people. The Kapawanamyu case, the first carbon farming initiative in the Aboriginal world, is an exemplar of these developments.

The Upper Cadell River in western Arnhem Land is one of the sites of an unbroken tradition of Aboriginal 'fire-stick farming'. The Australian continent has been shaped by wildfires for millions of years. These fires were controlled by Aboriginal people using fire across vast landscapes in a mosaic pattern of burning that reduced the vegetation after each monsoonal wet season. These ancient practices had almost ceased in northern Australia as a result of the policy of assimilation that included bringing Aboriginal populations into small townships in the 1950s. The traditional Aboriginal owners of the Upper Cadell River re-established their community at Kapawanamyu, and, from this base, they worked with Bawinanga rangers from the Maningrida township, land management expert Peter Cooke, other scientists and researchers, and officers from the Northern Territory Parks and Wildlife Commission, to continue traditional controlled burning of their estates for biodiversity conservation purposes.

The Aboriginal tradition of controlled or mosaic burning is practised for various reasons. One is to protect particular vegetation communities. Small fires lit throughout the year by traditional owners protect woodlands, sandstone heath, and monsoonal rainforest enclaves, vine forests and riparian rainforest from wildfires. Another vegetation community that is deliberately protected by these fire traditions is the Cypress pine (*Callitris intratropica*) forests. These are endangered by spreading wildfires and remain only in the protected gorges of the high sandstone country. The condition of cypress stands indicates the severity of the wildfires – dead cypress stems indicate there have been high-intensity fires. No exotic weeds have been found in this area and Aboriginal people are able to continue their food-gathering practices in this rich environment.

This traditional knowledge has been deployed again in solving modern problems. Led by the late artist and traditional owner Wamut, researchers such as Peter Cooke and the Bawinanga rangers, the West

Arnhem Land Aboriginal community has become the partner in an innovative carbon abatement scheme. The West Arnhem Fire Management Agreement is a partnership between Aboriginal traditional owners, the Darwin Liquefied Natural Gas project and Indigenous representative organisations to implement strategic fire management across 28,000 square kilometres of western Arnhem Land for the purposes of offsetting some of the greenhouse gas emissions from the Liquefied Natural Gas plant at Wickham Point in Darwin Harbour. This is the first such development in what promises to be an important niche for Aboriginal people in the 'green economy'.

My history of these developments is necessarily a patchwork of selected events. There are many people to honour in this history: John Koowarta and Koiki Eddie Mabo, Wamut, as well as other visionary Aboriginal leaders like them. There are also the visionary researchers and scientists who learnt from men and women like Wamut. Their love of nature and science was tempered with lessons from the Aboriginal world. Wamut was inducted from an early age in an ancient knowledge system that underpinned millennia of land and biodiversity management. Peter Cooke, whom I have mentioned, worked with Wamut, and through four decades of living in the Aboriginal world, was able to provide western skills of research and science, leading to the outstanding example of this first Aboriginal carbon-farming scheme. It is a model for other Aboriginal people to be inspired by, so that they too can forge partnerships with scientists and industry to create similar carbon abatement schemes and carbon trading businesses.

For more than 200 years the 'legal fiction' of *terra nullius* rendered native title, Aboriginal land law and Aboriginal persons as landowners under that law invisible at Australian law. This notion of an 'empty continent', finally rejected in 1992 in the High Court decision in the Mabo case, assumed that there was no one to conquer. Indigenous people, by the stroke of a judicial pen, reappeared as persons with law and proprietary rights, or at least possessory rights. The dismissal of the concept of *terra nullius* from legal assumptions about land law has caused Indigenous people to expect that relationships based on justice are possible, relationships which will write Indigenous people fully into the modern history of the state.

Aboriginal people and their land management traditions have also been rendered invisible in the Australian environment by the 'wilderness' discourse and its 'science fictions'. Some of these are sourced in racist mythology and others from the assumption of the superiority of western knowledge over Indigenous knowledge systems, the result of which is, often, a failure to recognise the critical relevance of these latter to sustainable environmental management.

One 'science fiction' is the widely held assumption that the northern Aboriginal and Torres Strait Islander terrestrial and marine domains should be categorised as 'wilderness' on the basis that no economic development or introduction of technological infrastructure has occurred in these areas. Another is that the Aboriginal owners do not desire development on their land, or that their wishes are irrelevant.

Until the debates about the use of the term in the Australian context were taken up in a public policy context in the 1990s, most popular usage of the term 'wilderness' in Australia had the effect of denying the imprint of millennia of Aboriginal impacts on, and relationships with, species and ecologies in Australian environmental history. The term, particularly as it is popularly used, has the effect of denying the very existence of Aboriginal biogeography. While perhaps not wittingly used to imply that this continent was devoid of human habitation and governance as meant by the pre-Mabo 'legal fiction' of *terra nullius,* it has nevertheless been a device to target Aboriginal land in a form of ecological imperialism. From 1991, there was Aboriginal protestation at the official use of this term as thousands of hectares of Aboriginal land were arbitrarily classified under the IUCN category of 'Wilderness Area' by officials and academics on the other side of the continent and across the seas.

In categorising Aboriginal land as 'wilderness', these zealots prejudice Aboriginal land interests by deeming them to have a non-title-related purpose, that is, the conservation of 'wilderness'. The bitter irony is that non-Aboriginal land titles, because of their history of predominantly unsustainable and destructive land uses, are not classified as 'wilderness' and their future use is not therefore limited by this device of classification.

They also ignore the gift of the first Australians to the world: 30 million hectares of protected areas to conserve environments and biodiversity, making up a quarter of the entire conservation-dedicated Reserve System in Australia, while Aboriginal people represent less than 3 per cent of the population.

There have been worthy attempts to re-define the term 'wilderness' to indicate a shift in scientific and policy thinking towards explicit recognition of the patchwork of multiple land uses within the Aboriginal domain, both customary and non-customary, and the value of integrating scientific and Indigenous systems of knowledge for responsible land management regimes. The survey, *Wilderness in Australia*, by Robertson, Vang and Brown, provides one of the very few explicit acknowledgements of colonial disturbance in their definition of 'wilderness'. They write:

> ... a wilderness area is therefore defined as an area that is, or is capable of being restored to be:
>
> of sufficient size to enable the long term preservation of its natural systems and biological diversity;
>
> substantially undisturbed by colonial and modern technological society; and
>
> remote at its core from points of mechanised access and other evidence of colonial and modern technological society.[25]

This approach to the idea of wilderness demonstrated that there were those who acknowledged the imprint of Aboriginal people in Australian landscapes and their ancient stewardship of this continent. This was a welcome development that gave grounds for common cause between traditional owners and scientists who established collaborative conservation research and management projects. The Aboriginal objections to the term 'wilderness' do not, of course, constitute an objection to the protection of natural values, but rather a demand for recognition of the cultural content of biophysical landscapes and the extent of the interdependence of cultural and natural values, at least in those landscapes where there has been almost uninterrupted Aboriginal management for millennia, such as in Arnhem Land.

There are true conservationists who understand the complexity of our natural world, who are informed by science, whether it is Aboriginal traditional knowledge or western science – and then there are the so-called 'wilderness' campaigners who abuse the trust placed in them by a gullible public. I never cease to be astonished at their ridiculous claim that Aborigines extinguished the megafauna and the claim that, thousands of years later, after colonisation of our continent, it is we who are the environmental vandals. The plain fact is that the vast majority of species extinctions occurred following the British invasion, and accelerated during the twentieth century. One might wonder how it is that they can ignore this undeniable fact. I have no explanation for this. Social media messages to me about this issue shortly after delivering this lecture as the fourth in the Boyer Lecture series in December 2012 reveal a deep-seated hatred of Aboriginal people as a fundamental tenet of their 'environmental' beliefs.

Much of this hatred is homegrown Australian racism expressed through the discourse of environmentalism. In my view, some of it has evolved from extremist adoption of the highly contentious, speculative and unproved claim that Flannery published in 1994.[26] It is impossible to ignore the racialised scientific endeavour in Australia and the persistence of ideas based on the scientism of 'race'. In the last 200 years, urbanisation, agriculture, pastoralism, industrialisation and other development have worked radical changes on the distinctive Australian environments, environments shaped and stewarded by the first Australians. These changes were based on the conquest of Aboriginal peoples on the frontiers. Construed as 'the vanishing race' by a nineteenth-century idea, Aboriginal people remain under threat from the romantic, but highly dangerous, ideas peddled by some conservationist campaigners.

FIVE

THE NEW NARRATIVE OF
INDIGENOUS SUCCESS

Australia's mining wealth has had varied impacts on our economy and the incomes of Australians. While there is no uniformity, it is clear that the result has raised the income levels of a large majority. Aboriginal people have not been exempt from this development. And with this new economic status has come social and political change.

I have been counting our victories against the racialist tendency in this society, the tendency of the settler state to destroy or control or warp any Aboriginal initiative. This is not a report card, but a simple count of present electoral successes: Ken Wyatt's seat in the House of Representatives; Linda Burney's long record in the New South Wales Parliament; Ben Wyatt's and Carol Martin's seats in the Legislative Assembly of Western Australia; and the four seats in the Northern Territory Assembly held by Alison Anderson, Larisa Lee, Francis Xavier Kurrupuwu, and Bess Nungarrayi Price. These successes reflect not just demography but increasing political sophistication among both Aboriginal people and the political class in Australia. The preparedness of the electorate to accept Indigenous Australians as political representatives who, unlike Pauline Hanson, represent their electorate regardless of race, is a great advance on the state of affairs in the 1960s, the time of my coming of age, when we did not have the right to vote, and were excluded from all national affairs by several racist provisions in the Constitution.[1]

There *are* general report cards on our status developed under the banner of the federal government's 'Close the Gap' campaign, designed to measure progress in overcoming various types of Aboriginal disadvantage in education, health, employment and other socioeconomic categories. The measurement of our status using these criteria encompasses many institutions, researchers, agencies, and different methodologies and approaches, all with varying degrees of sophistication and accuracy. Annually, the federal Parliament receives the Productivity Commission's Report on Indigenous disadvantage, and the Aboriginal and Torres Strait Islander Social Justice Commissioner's Social Justice Report. These are essential reading for obtaining a current picture of the state of affairs. The problem with the report card approach, however, is that it is not required to tell us what caused various measurements to shift up or down the scale.

In these lectures, I have paraphrased fifty years of change in the relationship between Aboriginal people and the mining industry, and the complex historical, social and economic factors at work. During this same period, similar trajectories of radical change have occurred in other spheres, including the overarching relationship between the nation state and Indigenous people, measured by constitutional and legal change.

In recent years, especially with the involvement of Indigenous people in the media, there is more reporting of success. If the conventional mainstream media were the only source of our understanding of these issues, we would be terminally depressed and pessimistic. Many Australians do have a pessimistic, not to say jaded, view of the status of Aboriginal people. We read simplistic comments from uninformed readers of newspapers regularly: 'If they worked like the rest of us, they would have nothing to whinge about.' 'Why should taxpayers support these bludgers?' These are the questions asked by our citizens bunkered in the suburbs where no Aboriginal footprint has been seen for more than a hundred years. They read about the budget expenditure on the mysterious category 'Indigenous Affairs' and imagine that cheques are being mailed out to individual Aboriginal people on a weekly basis.

Such naïve views reflect the general unawareness of the actual nature of the 'Indigenous Affairs' machine. It exists to measure, to categorise and to report. It is administered largely by well-paid white people. Their business is not to write cheques, but to write memos and reports. If they do activate the cheque-writing processes in the bureaucracy, they do so more often to pay the army of consultants producing feasibility reports and evaluations. I receive letters and emails from people of goodwill who are trying to do something positive, and who have tried to engage with the 'Indigenous Affairs' machine. They come away with scathing views of the roundabout of bureaucrats, agencies, websites, application forms and absurd meetings. I have talked to Aboriginal people who have registered with an agency to find employment. Their stories are accounts of Kafkaesque horror. I have my own experiences of being trapped in the dark corridors of this machine, tracking my way through the maze of bureaucracy and papers that seem to reproduce like cancer cells.

Counting the successes, then, is a pleasant pastime that sometimes results in a small measure of hope in a landscape of obstacles, bureaucratic monsters and traps.

We should not count our progress by measuring it one step after another. The problem is far too complex for that. But one statistic has given me some cause for hope. Professor Ian Anderson, an Aboriginal medical specialist, told me that, in 2012, enrolments of Indigenous people in first year medical studies have reached national parity with the non-Indigenous student enrolments. This statistic tells me so much. I began these lectures by referring to the emergence of an Aboriginal middle class, a phenomenon that has been ignored by the professionals paid to observe and measure our lives. This statistic is an instance of the wellbeing experienced by those Aboriginal and Torres Strait Islander families. Their accumulation of social and human capital in the space of perhaps one, but no more than three generations, has enabled them to send their children to university to study medicine.

This development does not sit well in the standard analysis of the Aboriginal 'problem' or the domain of 'Indigenous Affairs'. Most of the protagonists in the intellectual workforce supported by the 'Indigenous Affairs' machine will ignore or refute this singularly important statistic. A few anthropologists have accused me of being a 'conservative', a 'neoliberal advocate for assimilation', of being incapable of 'objectivity' by virtue of being Aboriginal. They are bound up in a sense of the discipline that I do not share. Theirs leads to a closed system of thought and does not allow Aboriginal agency in the events I have described. Only a handful have a clear sense of the rapid changes in Aboriginal economic participation, while the protagonists for an outmoded theoretical mode are flailing about in the death throes of an intellectual paradigm that offers a weak explanation, if any at all, of the statistics concerning the demographic reality of a predominantly young population and all the disadvantages, discrimination and challenges these young people face; nor do they admit Indigenous achievements in, for instance, medicine, law, media, and other fields, and the implications of a growing band of competent, educated Aboriginal professionals for Aboriginal society as a whole. These professionals are engaged with the challenges of modernity, expertly challenging and dismissing the old shibboleths about Aboriginal advancement. This is a robust engagement that is incrementally and surely changing the way business is done in more open, less circumscribed and regulated communities. By contrast, a small but vocal group of the Australianist anthropologists is dependent, financially and professionally, on the old paradigm of the static, immutable, and above all subaltern, Aboriginal society, and some of them, in their online discussions, express contempt for Aboriginal people who rise above their station. Their contribution has been to inform the policy statis and general tolerance of poverty and misery in the Aboriginal world with a peculiar narrative about a very restricted and increasingly rare type of Aboriginal society.

Poverty, alienation and disadvantage in the Aboriginal community, and the history of settler–Aboriginal relations, have triggered several intellectual movements and fashions in the last fifty years. I have described the return of the 'noble savage' concept in the wilderness conservation movement in previous lectures. Variations on ideas in the late Robert Hughes's tome *The Culture of Complaint*[2] bemoaning the impact of movements based on historical grievance were fashionable for a while, and so too was Keith Windschuttle's ridiculous book *The Fabrication of Aboriginal History*.[3] There were snide remarks and published tomes from anthropologists and ethnographers about 'designer tribalism'[4] and a new language for race hate emerged, enthusiastically taken up by opinion columnists and shock jocks Alan Jones, Andrew Bolt, Piers Akerman and many others. Windschuttle was joined by other rabid denialists of the fate of Aboriginal people in Australian history – especially in relation to the stolen generations – such as the late Paddy McGuinness, editor of *Quadrant*, Piers Akerman of Sydney's *Daily Telegraph*, and Andrew Bolt of Melbourne's *Herald Sun*. Their specious refutations of the removal of Aboriginal children, of massacres and injustices have not survived a decade, and history will treat them with the contempt they deserve.

There are other monsters stalking this landscape and one of them is a favourite of the professional dissidents in the Aboriginal movement: 'Aboriginal sovereignty'. There is a small and powerful group of Aboriginal people involved in the politics of this domain, stridently advocating this concept. What does it mean? A separate state? Enactment of Indigenous rights? Such questions have never been answered, and the concept remains a slogan, one that points to a vaporous dream of self-determination but does not require any actual activity in the waking world to materialise it. It is Australia's version of the Marcus Garvey movement of 1950s Jamaica that dreamt of the repatriation of African descendants to Africa and involved the proto-Rastafarians in rituals such as waiting on the wharf for their saviour, Emperor Haile Selassie of Ethiopia, to arrive on a ship and rescue them. In the early 1990s, some advocates for this idea of Aboriginal sovereignty had Aboriginal passports made and with them travelled internationally for some years. When Prime Minister John Howard learnt about it, he was enraged, and made telephone calls to investigate. A very senior corporate executive called me to ask what he should tell the prime minister. I told him to say that their Aboriginal sovereignty passport stunt was designed to make themselves attractive to women, such as the groupies that hang around at international forums on Indigenous rights. It was a joke that wasn't funny. It bemuses me that so many people are enthralled by this absurd political ideology. In 1995, Noel Pearson tried to refute it with plain logic. He said:

> In a world crumbling in the face of the inability of
> peoples to come to terms with historical grievance

and our inability to locate and respect group rights to self-determination within the concept of a unified and peaceful nation – I believe that the only choice available to both indigenous and non-indigenous Australians is to find a way of living together in a unified community which respects our particular and different identities and the particular rights of indigenous peoples. Because, as I often say to the occasional discomfort of both black and white people, Mabo has put to rest two gross fantasies. Firstly, it has put to rest the fantasy that the blacks were not and are still not here. The fantasy of terra and homo nullius. Secondly, Mabo also puts to rest the fantasy that the whites are somehow going to pack up and leave. Coexistence remains our lot.[5]

There is an undercurrent in the Reconciliation movement that has gone unnoticed. At public events over the last twenty years, many Aboriginal advocates of reconciliation have addressed themselves not to the settlers who want absolution for their ancestral past in Australia's history, but to young Aboriginal people attracted to the Aboriginal sovereignty slogans. They have tried to deter them from taking a fatuous political path and encourage them towards one with ideas and activities that will improve their lives and sense of self-esteem. For all my cynicism about Reconciliation and those who co-opt the idea to mask the same old intentions of keeping Aborigines in their place as permanent subalterns, I have respect for those messages from the wise old warriors who brought about the changes during the civil rights era of the 1960s and 1970s.

The message has been received. I heard Neil Willmett, Aboriginal businessman, president of the Indigenous Business Council, and publisher of the *Aboriginal Business Magazine*, say at a conference that he was following in the footsteps of his elders who established the Aboriginal medical and legal services in the 1970s. Like them, he is involved in building an institution to assist Aboriginal people. He reminded us that Aboriginal people had established businesses on the Australian frontiers during colonial times, and told a story of his own ancestors in Queensland, who were stripped of their property by the state at a time when it was illegal for Aboriginal people to own property and to engage in business. His campaign for Aboriginal business strength is a continuation of the long civil rights movement.

Noel Pearson challenged principal advocate of Aboriginal sovereignty Michael Mansell and his entourage to develop an ideological consciousness 'that goes beyond absolutist, nihilist daydreaming about what should be, but instead become concerned with how we are actually going to go about making things the way they should be'.

Pearson's Cape York agenda over the past twenty years stands in stark contrast to the futile activism of the professional Aboriginal dissidents who cling to their own form of Garveyism. Their ship has not come in, and they have deceived too many of our young people. But not all.

I have been thrilled by the *Redfern Now* television series on ABC Television, broadcast during the time I was writing these lectures. Produced by Rachel Perkins and her team at Blackfella Films, with a magnificent team of Indigenous writers, directors, actors and technicians in collaboration with famous English scriptwriter Jimmy McGovern and a range of partners, it speaks to the Aboriginal people who have lived through these turgid political dramas. It depicts the emergence of an Aboriginal middle class with veracity, its members intimately linked to their families living on the Block in Redfern, and the transference of Aboriginal cultural values from the Block to the suburbs. It shows Aboriginal values and social practices at work in dramatic scenes of encounters with the police, the struggle of families to deter youth from criminal activities, and the trauma of dealing with mental illness.

In Episode 1, 'Family', Leah Purcell's character sacrifices a family holiday in Bali to care for her sister's children when the sister's world falls apart in a psychotic episode. The battle of loyalties and values was brilliantly portrayed. Those who have joined the workforce and earned some of the privileges and assets that most Australians take for granted are not entirely free to enjoy them while others in their family might not have been able to improve their circumstances. The bonds of kinship tie families dispersing across Australian cities and towns in a cobweb of ancient traditions and modern dilemmas.

Artists such as Rachel Perkins and her exceptional team members have done a far better job than anthropologists and political ideologues in describing these challenges. With minute attention to the intimate details of Aboriginal life at the Block and the tendrils of familial, social and political connection across geography, class and history, they have broadcast more truth and sociological sophistication into Australian homes than thousands of papers from the intellectual militias of the 'Indigenous Affairs' machine.

Those of us who have raged against the machine and won a few successes know that the challenge lies in large part in capturing the hearts and minds of young people with a message of hope. The future that they must imagine for themselves must come not from the false dreams of Garveyism but from opportunities to enable them to live a good life. This is why Noel Pearson's Welfare Reform Project and education initiatives are so important and effective in transforming the lives of people in Cape York. The inspiration Noel has given to others across the country should not be underestimated. In the face of the rancorous denials from the band of Noel Pearson haters, the facts keep stacking up. The majority of Aboriginal leaders have adopted similar strategies to Pearson's. Ben Wyatt, the member for Victoria Park in Western Australia, gave a speech in November 2012 that traverses the points made by Noel Pearson a decade ago. Noel denounced 'the soft bigotry of low expectations', citing American President Lyndon B. Johnson's comment during the civil rights era. Ben Wyatt denounced government policy based on 'palliative economics – a defeatist attitude premised on Aboriginal culture dying'. He said: 'No longer is it acceptable to view regional poverty from the social welfare perspective'; 'palliative economics must be replaced by building relationships between indigenous communities and industry'; 'Aboriginal people cannot be empowered if they are not willing to prioritise the one key to empowerment – education'; 'If we do not accept that a school in a regional or remote part of Western Australia must perform at mainstream standards, then what is the point of that school? How are we providing Indigenous empowerment with such expectations?'; 'We cannot deliver a standard of education lower than what we expect in Perth and then expect "mainstream" jobs to flow. We are, effectively, giving Governmental endorsement to a 'palliative education' system'.[6]

A younger generation of Aboriginal people are telling stories through literature, the arts, film and music, and speaking about history and oppression without the burden of the culture wars. *Redfern Now*, *The Sapphires*, directed by Wayne Blair, *Toomelah*, directed by Ivan Sen, and *Samson and Delilah*, directed by Warwick Thornton, are just some examples of their outpouring of creative work, thinking and writing. While several Aboriginal films have been selected for the Cannes Film Festival and won awards around the globe, in a first for an Australian Indigenous director, *The Sapphires* will be distributed internationally by American producer Harvey Weinstein's company.

Indigenous filmmakers and television producers have cemented their place in the mainstream, winning over audiences and proving their box office success.

They are confident and refuse to be stereotyped. They want to keep some of our cultural traditions and they reject others. They abhor the abuse caused by alcohol and drugs, but they have compassion for the abusers. They want hope. Recently, I asked Warwick Thornton if the non-Aboriginal audience for *Samson and Delilah* were deluding themselves when they believed it to be a story of hope. In the denouement of this powerful drama his principal characters, a petrol sniffer and his girlfriend, who is a victim of rape, retreat to an outstation with little likelihood of a happy ending. His answer was this: 'If they believe that they can live for one more day, then there is hope.'

What do these extraordinary Aboriginal storytellers – Perkins, Thornton, Blair and many others – have in common? They are educated. They are successful. They are proud of their Aboriginal heritage. They glow with self-esteem. And their ability to tell these gripping stories through award-winning film and television productions comes from their intimate understanding of Aboriginal life, whether in Redfern or Papunya, Toomelah or Cummeragunga. What is also remarkably similar throughout their work is their view of the Aboriginal dilemma in the struggle with modernity. On the one hand there is the backdrop of the scourge of colonial history, alcohol and drug abuse, the vulnerability of youth in dysfunctional family settings, the constant racism and police presence; and on the other, the resilience of Aboriginal people that sometimes results in a victory, small or large, against the odds. Cultural values and kinship bonds are not by themselves the source of victory; they are sometimes the cause of anguish and conflicted values, of threats to survival, catching the young in a web of alcohol and drug dependency, demand-sharing and self-exclusion from the opportunities in the wider world. But these cultural values also strengthen their will to survive. They find self-esteem in celebrating their cultural identity and heritage. Youthful desire for adventure, to go out into the world for new experiences, to climb a metaphoric mountain or catch a dream; these are universal. What Aboriginal youth experience is not so different from their counterparts in Brazil or Africa or Timor Leste, all places where old traditions and rapid change clash too.

The details vary, and sometimes considerably, but these stories of young dreams are the stuff of the human dilemma that most settler Australians or their ancestors left behind in their original homelands. Dickens' novels, such as *Oliver Twist*, are rich with analogies to these postmodern tales of poverty, hunger, hierarchies, repression, exploitation, and the desire for something better. It is colonialism and racism rather than class that mark these stories as different. The impacts of the end of feudalism in England, the land tenure revolution and the industrial mills of Dickens' England are similar in many ways to those of the mines of 21st-century Australia; and, also similar in their power to transform societies and economies.

What I have marvelled at in this heady mix of social change is the resilience of Aboriginal culture. The threat that the old racists, leftists and Aboriginal sovereignty advocates level against the new Aboriginal intellectuals is a prediction that Aboriginal culture will 'die out'. Aboriginal culture has changed dramatically in many parts of Australia, but it survives, as the works of our filmmakers and artists demonstrate. The most important thing is that it is viable, supported more and more not by the welfare state but by the engagement of entrepreneurs, artists, filmmakers and workers in the economy, and the accrual by the first generation of private material wealth.

I spoke to one of my Aboriginal friends at Perth airport recently. He is a successful businessman, and he was heading home to attend Aboriginal law ceremonies for the next three months because, he said, 'the old people may not be around for much longer'. These ceremonies will be held not far from the mines about which I have spoken. Aboriginal men and women have dedicated some proportion of this new social capital to cultural maintenance and renewal, and made Aboriginal endeavours commercially viable. Our culture is no longer simply a country for anthropologists, New Age mystics and wilderness campaigners to colonise. Their tragic, necrophiliac and self-serving accounts are no competition for the works of the new guard of Aboriginal creative workers, nor for actual Aboriginal culture.

Economic factors have made this possible, just as much as the factors that have contributed to our cultural resilience. Ben Wyatt's point about 'palliative economics' is most timely. The grasp of the welfare state, the protectionist state that addresses itself to an old paradigm of the mendicant natives, is loosening. A new generation of Aboriginal people is turning dreams into reality: education, economic participation, self-esteem and success are part of this new Aboriginal world, and there is no going back.

ENDNOTES

Introduction

1   cf. Atkinson W., 'Mediating the Mindset of Opposition: The Yorta Yorta case', *Indigenous Law Bulletin*, 5 (15), 2002; Neate G., 'Native Title Ten years On: Getting on with the job or sitting on the fence?', www.nntt.gov.au/news-and-communications/speeches-and-papers/documents/2002/speeches%20nt%20ten%20years%20on%20neate%20may%202002.pdf.

2   See www.atns.net.au.

3   These include consent determinations and Indigenous Land Use Agreements involving issues of native title; see the National Native Title Tribunal website at www.nntt.gov.au/Pages/default.aspx for a comprehensive list of native title determinations.

4   See, for example, Argyle Diamond Mine Participation Agreement: Management Plan Agreement.

5   See, for example, the Yorta Yorta Co-operative Management Agreement.

6   Australian Government Department of Industry, Tourism and Resources, 'Working with Indigenous Communities', Leading practice sustainable development program for the mining industry, Canberra, 2007.

7   Ibid.

8   World Business Council for Sustainable Development,
     Corporate Social Responsibility: Making good business sense,
     World Business Council for Sustainable Development, 2000,
     p. 9.

9   Charlie Lenegan (Managing Director, Rio Tinto), 'The
     Minerals Sector and Indigenous Relations', paper presented
     at the Resourcing and Innovative Industry – Minerals Week
     2005, 30 May–3 June 2005 Hyatt Hotel and Parliament
     House, Canberra.

10   O'Fairchealleagh, C., 'Negotiating Major Project Agreements:
     The Cape York Model''', discussion paper no. 11, Australian
     Institute for Aboriginal and Torres Strait Islander Studies,
     2000, p. 1.

11   See Langton, M., *Burning Questions*, Centre for Indigenous
     Natural and Cultural Resource Management, Northern
     Territory University, Darwin, 1994.

12   Tim Flannery, *Quarterly Essay: After the future, Australia's
     new extinction crisis,* p. 33.

13   Professor Flannery said he had been misunderstood. "In
     writing that national parks are not 'safe', I meant that they are
     not secure as a permanent part of the national parks estate.
     I expressed no view whether biodiverisity would be more or
     less secure under indigenous management ... biodiversity has
     done best where NGOs and indigenous groups have worked,"
     he said. *Sydney Morning Herald*, 8 December 2012.

14   Bowman, D.M.J.S., 'The Impact of Aboriginal Landscape
     Burning on the Australian Biota' in *New Phytologist*, vol. 140,
     no. 3, 1998, p. 3.

**ONE Faustian bargain or survival strategy? Mining and
Aboriginal economic empowerment**

1   The evidence of an emerging middle class comes from many
     sources and analysing various types of data relating to

educational and employment achievements, home ownership and other factors that contribute to increasing income, wellbeing and capacity to participate in the Australian society and economy. The Australian Bureau of Statistics has reported very little information pertaining to Indigenous Australians from the most recent census. By itself, without additional research and analysis, ABS data can be misleading. Most reports on Indigenous status relate to the ABS 2002 and 2008 National Aboriginal and Torres Strait Islander Survey. The common practice in demographic and statistical analysis is to report on rates of disadvantage but there are a few examples of reporting of trends of increasing wellbeing in our population. One, for example, is the ABS report on Education and Indigenous Wellbeing (but note that this is based on 1994, 2002 and 2008 data):

> In 2008, 37% of Aboriginal and Torres Strait Islander people aged 18 years and over (adults) had attained a minimum of Year 12 or a skilled vocational qualification, more than double the rate in 1994 (16%). Over the same time period, those completing a minimum of Year 10 or basic vocational qualifications increased from 48% to 71%. While relatively few Aboriginal and Torres Strait Islander adults continued on to complete a Bachelor degree or above, the rate has increased to 5% in 2008 … Attainment of higher levels of education was more common among adults living in Major Cities than those living in Regional and Remote Areas. In 2008, for example, adults living in Major Cities were three times as likely to have attained a Bachelor degree or above (9%).(http:www.abs.gov. au/socialtrends, Indigenous Education and WellBeing, Australian Bureau of Statistics, Catalogue no. 4102.0)

Taken together with other data on employment outcomes and homeownership, this data on educational achievement

outcomes is evidence of a small but growing number of
Indigenous people participating in Australian society in the
same way as 'middle class' Australians. The principal point
being made here is that not all Indigenous Australians fit the
standard stereotype of the poor, undereducated, unemployed
and disempowered Aboriginal person reported on regularly
in the media and which informs policymakers, educators and
police, who generally treat all Aboriginal people according to
this stereotype.

2 Eminent Australian anthropologist W.E.H. Stanner (1905–
1981) wrote several scholarly publications dealing with
Aboriginal religion (e.g. *On Aboriginal Religion*, 1989) while
his popular works, such as the essays published in *White
Man Got No Dreaming* (1979), deal with a variety of subjects
relating to the changes in Aboriginal society he had observed.
While the public might have been persuaded mistakenly to
believe in a 'primordium', or original human society, by his
marvellous accounts of Aboriginal religion, and reached
perhaps some kind of understanding of the radical difference
that Aboriginal religion presented, they would have largely
remained ignorant of his views on the economic changes
gripping Aboriginal society. In his essay on his informant
and friend Durmugam, with whom he lived in the Daly River
area during his fieldwork stints, Stanner gave an explanation
of the Aborigines' 'sound calculus' of dispensing with the
rigours and deprivation of the hunting and gathering life
in their much impaired homelands in favour of European
foodstuffs and especially the addictive tea and tobacco
paid to them for manual labour. Stanner was the master of
the neologism, and his term 'squeeze-play' remains apt in
designating the stratagems used by Aboriginal people locked
out of the wealth creation and economic activity around them
to obtain a few advantages by politicking and manipulating

a heartless system. He summarised his understanding of the economic basis of the culture change occurring at that time: 'The blacks have grasped eagerly at any possibility of a regular and dependable food supply for a lesser effort than is involved in nomadic hunting and foraging … a persistent and positive effort to make themselves dependent' on the peanut farmers along the river.' 'I appreciated the good sense of the adaptation,' he wrote, 'only after I had gone hungry from fruitless hunting with rifle, gun and spears in one of the best environments in Australia.' (Marcia Langton, Chronicles of a disaster foretold, in *Australian Literary Review*, 4 March 2009; see also 'Durmugam, A Nangiomeri', in Casagrande, J.B., *In the Company of Man; Twenty Portraits of Anthropological Informants*, 1964).

3   The modern proponents of wilderness protection often dichotomise Aborigines into two extremes: the 'new noble savage' in harmony with the environment and the modern Aborigine who poses the threat of extinction to rare and endangered species by virtue of wearing shoes, driving a Toyota and hunting with guns. The first High Court finding on the characteristics of an Aboriginal person was in the Franklin Dam case in which environmentalists and archaeologists were pitted against Tasmanian Aboriginal people who did not fit the caricature of the noble savage who was imagined to have inhabited the caves of the so-called Tasmanian wilderness. That finding in the High Court decision on the Franklin Dam Case revealed acutely for the first time that the Australian use of the term 'wilderness' was a mystification of genocide. Where Aboriginal people had been brought to the brink of annihilation, their former territories were recast as 'wilderness'.

One astonishing example of the arbitrary classification of Aboriginal land for conservation purposes is set out in C.

Michael Hall's *Wasteland to World Heritage* (1992), in which he shows all Aboriginal land, including all of Arnhem Land, as 'minor wilderness'.

Most popular usage of the term 'wilderness' in Australia has had the effect of denying the imprint of millennia of Aboriginal impacts on, and relationships with, species and ecologies in Australian environmental history. The term is used to infer, perhaps not wittingly, that this continent was devoid of human habitation and governance as meant by the pre-Mabo legal fiction of *terra nullius*. It is for this reason that there was Aboriginal protestation at the official use of this term as thousands of hectares of Aboriginal land were arbitrarily classified under the International Union for Conservation of Nature category of 'Wilderness Area' by officials and academics on the other side of the continent and across the seas.

There is a widely held assumption that the northern Aboriginal and Torres Strait Islander terrestrial and marine domains should be categorised as 'wilderness' on the basis that no economic development or introduction of technological infrastructure has occurred in these areas. In categorising Aboriginal land as 'wilderness', environmental planners and scholars target these areas as eligible for inclusion in the reserve system, or 'a national wilderness system which gives legislative protection to wilderness areas' (Hall, 1992, p. 8). The National Wilderness Inventory is a peculiar device which constitutes a layering of non-proprietorial, but nevertheless restrictive, interests over the Australian land tenure system. In that it classifies most, if not all, Aboriginal land, whatever the title, as 'wilderness', it prejudices Aboriginal land interests (much more so than non-Aboriginal land interests), both customary and non-customary, by deeming them to have a non-title-related purpose, that is, the conservation of 'wilderness'. The Inventory thereby reduces the potential for future Aboriginal use of the land because of the history of conservative Aboriginal land use. The bitter irony is that non-Aboriginal land titles, because of their history of predominantly unsustainable and destructive land uses, are not classified as 'wilderness' and their future use is not therefore limited by this classificatory device.

4   'Welfare transfers', as I use the term here, are the social security payments paid by the Commonwealth government to individuals residing in an area or region, and which totalled as the sum of all payments to the region can be compared to other sources of income of those in the region. Such analyses are used to determine the extent of welfare dependency in a population and this is relevant to understanding poverty, or low income levels, so often related to a range of socioeconomic disadvantages. Income levels may be determinants, for instance, of rates of morbidity, contact with the criminal justice system, and mortality rates. Rather than use national data, such as Australian Bureau of Statistics figures, which in the case of small, dispersed Indigenous populations, misrepresent the situation in local or regional areas, I cite social scientists who have rigorously collected or analysed Indigenous income data to supplement and, sometimes, correct, the under-enumeration and other problems with ABS data. See, for instance, Taylor, J. & Scambary, B., *Indigenous People and the Pilbara Mining Boom: A baseline for regional participation*, research monograph no. 25, Centre for Aboriginal Economic Policy Research, Australian National University, 2005. See also: Tanuja Barker, *Employment outcomes for Aboriginal people: An exploration of experiences and challenges in the Australian minerals industry*, Centre For Social Responsibility In Mining

Research Paper No. 6, Centre for Social Responsibility in Mining, Sustainable Minerals Institute, University of Queensland, Australia, October 2006.

5   After the Referendum, the franchise was extended to Aboriginal people in some jurisdictions, such as Queensland, for instance. A flurry of legislative reform followed but there is insufficient space here for the full details. In South Australia, Aboriginal Land Trusts were established so that Aboriginal people had some legal and governance rights in lands that had been classified formerly as Aboriginal Reserves. The Commonwealth *Racial Discrimination Act 1975*, enacted during the term of the Whitlam government, provided limited protection to all Australians from racial discrimination and proved to be useful to Indigenous people in a range of cases. The Fraser government quickly asserted a commitment to Aboriginal self-management, passing a number of significant pieces of legislation which significantly worked to alter the state of affairs with regard to Indigenous people in Queensland and the Northern Territory. Undoubtedly the most significant of these was the *Aboriginal Land Rights (Northern Territory) Act 1976* which established a Territory-wide scheme for the granting of freehold title to Indigenous groups with claims to areas of land.

The second significant legislative enactment by the Fraser government was the *Aboriginal Community Act* 1979, which granted authority to certain Aboriginal communities in the Northern Territory to make by-laws with respect to a range of matters including entry onto community land and certain law and order matters with respect to the community.

New South Wales and Queensland later passed less robust legislation. The *Native Title Act* was enacted by the federal Parliament under Prime Minister Paul Keating in 1993 and commenced in 1994.

6   The fly-in fly-out shift rotations are challenging and up to two-thirds of this workforce find it difficult to stay on these contracts for more than a year despite the very high incomes. The impact on family life and health are two factors most often cited.

7   The health sector has provided the large majority of jobs taken by Indigenous people joining the workforce in the last two decades.

8   Taylor, J. & Scambary, B., *Indigenous People and the Pilbara Mining Boom: A baseline for regional participation*, research monograph no. 25, Centre for Aboriginal Economic Policy Research, Australian National University, 2005, p. 152.

9   The ethnic mix in regional Australia is changing quickly as the mining industry attracts workers from Australia and overseas into the outback. The generation of Australians that lived through the changes in the constitutional and legal status of Aboriginal people from the 1960s to the present time have reached the end of their working lives, and a new generation, born after the period when Indigenous people had no citizenship rights or special Indigenous rights, have little understanding of the history of that period.

10 In 1965 the Queensland Government granted a mining lease covering 5,500 square kilometres to Comalco, a lease area now reduced to 2,500 square kilometres until 2041, with the right of further extension for another twenty-one years. Weipa was built as a company town and is largely populated by non-Indigenous people who have relocated temporarily. It is connected by a daily jet service to Cairns (some 700 kilometres southeast) and by 1100 kilometres of unsealed road that is usually impassable from December to April. Bauxite is transported out of Weipa, and supplies come into it, through the Gulf of Carpentaria (Harvey, B., 'Rio Tinto's Agreement

Making in Australia in a Context of Globalisation', seminar paper in possession of the author).

11   On 13 March 1963 the government excised more than 300 square kilometres of land from the Arnhem Land reserve for the Nabalco bauxite mine. Yolngu people from the then Methodist mission at Yirrkala sent two bark petitions to the Commonwealth Parliament in August 1963 protesting the mine and asserting their traditional ownership of and rights to the land. In 1968, after their petitions to Parliament failed to gain recognition of their rights to land, Yolngu people from Yirrkala in eastern Arnhem Land took their case to the Northern Territory Supreme Court to assert their continuing ownership of traditional lands by challenging the validity of the Commonwealth government's grant of mining leases over their territory. Their battle was lost eight years later when Justice Blackburn found against them in this famous case that became known as the Gove Land Rights case (*Milirrpum v. Nabalco Pty Ltd*).

12   I refer the reader to a number of my publications that explain the legal rights that the *Native Title Act 1993* (*NTA*) affords particular Indigenous people and how these translate into economic rights, have done so, especially since the 1998 amendments to the *NTA*, and continue to do so. The agreements I refer to are Indigenous Land Use Agreements and S.31 agreements under the *NTA* and these are legally binding on the parties. See Agreements, Treaties and Negotiated Settlements Project website at www.atns. net.au/default.asp, which hosts an interactive website and database, and, for a summary of the issues, read the chapter by Langton, M.,& Webster, A., 'The Right to Negotiate, the Resources Industry, Agreements and the *Native Title Act*: A retrospective of Mabo's legacy' in Bauman, T. &

Glick, L., *The Limits of Change: Mabo and native title 20 years on*, Aboriginal Studies Press, Canberra, 2012; and my essay, 'Mining the Mabo Legacy' in the supplement *Some Provocations* to the *Griffith REVIEW*, edition 36 (*What is Australia For?*). Several chapters of Langton, M. & Longbottom, J. (eds), *Community Futures, Legal Architecture: Foundations for Indigenous people in the global mining boom*, Routledge (UK), 2012, would also be helpful.

13   At the time of finalising this book in January 2013, there were 620 Indigenous Land Use Agreements (ILUAs) recorded on the website of the Agreements, Treaties and Negotiated Settlements Project, www.atns.net.au/subcategory.asp?subcategoryID=121. These are registered with the National Native Title Tribunal.

TWO In from the cold: The emergence of the economic Aborigine

1   The *Racial Discrimination Act* was passed in 1975.

2   Tim Rowse's *White Flour, White Power* is a compelling history of the role of food politics in the sedentarisation and control of Aboriginal populations in Central Australia. Rowse's close reading of the sources results in a detailed picture of the transition from the original economy to one of managed consumption and dependence on rations under an increasingly centralised ration system. At first implementing rationing to secure contact and trust, and later, to prevent Aborigines spearing cattle, the colonial administrators and settlers were forced to expand the distribution of rations with the onset of drought. With little choice but to congregate and wait for rations, Aboriginal people were drawn to the pastoral stations, 'where their natural food supply is materially, if intermittently augmented by the refuse of the slaughter yard, or even by gifts of entire beasts' (Rowse, T., *White Flour, White Power: From rations to citizenship in Central Australia*,

Cambridge University Press, Cambridge (UK), 1998, p. 15, citing E.C. Stirling, 'Anthropology' in *Report on the Work of the Horn Scientific Expedition to Central Australia*, Dulau and Co., London, Melville & Slade, Melbourne, vol. 4, no. 7, 1896.)

In Queensland, for similar reasons, the police, and later Protectors and Sub-Protectors, also issued rations from the 1880s, and the ration system had become extensive by the late 1890s. The distribution of government-funded rations to Aboriginal people in northern Queensland occurred through missions, settler stations and government food-relieving centres. A 'no work no food' regime was also followed at many missions to reduce reliance on irregular government rations and to attract and maintain the local Aboriginal people as a permanent working community. The intention was to 'civilise' them and train them in Christian ways of living. In his 1896 report, Meston comments on the barren soil of Aboriginal missions: 'Some evil genius seems to have presided over the selection of sites for all the Mission Stations in Queensland.' Pertinent examples include Cape Bedford, Bloomfield, Mapoon, Weipa and Aurukun. Most locations therefore relied on government rations for some, if not all, of their subsistence. However, government rations were irregular and often inadequate.

3   As historian Ros Kidd demonstrates for the situation in Queensland, Aboriginal wages were confiscated, either partially or wholly, to fund state development. There is a wealth of literature on the 'stolen wages'. See for instance, Standing Committee on Legal and Constitutional Affairs, 'Unfinished Business: Indigenous stolen wages', December 2006; Kidd, R., *The Way We Civilise: Aboriginal affairs: The untold story*, University of Queensland Press, St Lucia, Qld, 1997; 'Black Lives: Deficits of the past or deceits of the present: Defining Aboriginal disadvantagement' in *Southern*

Review, vol. 31, no 1, 1998, pp. 11–17; *Black Lives, Government Lies, Frontlines, Sydney,* University of New South Wales Press, Kensington, NSW, 2000.

4   Until 1908, the Commonwealth offered its citizens no social security to ease the hardships in times of old age and invalidity. Some states had pension schemes. Seven years after federation, national aged and invalid pension schemes were enacted, and in 1912, maternity allowances. However, 'Aboriginal Natives' were disqualified from all payments. Throughout the Great Depression, Indigenous people continued to be excluded from eligibility for any benefit. After the World War II, a comprehensive and universal system of social security existed in Australia, except for Aborigines. The first payment to which Indigenous people had access was a child endowment payment introduced in 1941. In 1942, 'Aboriginal Natives' became eligible for Commonwealth pensions, but as the Racial Discrimination Commissioner pointed out, the 1942 amendments excluded 'Aboriginal Natives' who were covered by the 'provisions of a state or territory law relating to the control of Aboriginal natives.' There were also exclusions for Indigenous people who were deemed 'nomadic' or 'primitive' and, despite the existence of entitlements: '. . . Social Security Act continued to discriminate against Aborigines by adding amendments that restricted access to pensions and allowance payments and placing Aboriginal Australians under the control of non-Aboriginal administered Aboriginal departments, missions, settlements and pastoral properties.'

    This policy of racist exclusion persisted until the late 1960s. In 1966, the Department of Social Services decided to remove all specific references to Aboriginal people from the *Social Security Act* including the provisions that disqualified 'Aboriginal Natives' who were nomadic or primitive. Despite this, the exclusion concerning Indigenous people living on government and mission stations persisted until 1976. Indigenous people living in remote communities continued to be excluded from participation in Australia's social security system well into the 1970s. A 'work test' was invented to exclude Aboriginal people in remote communities from unemployment benefits, living and other social security benefits. As wards of the state or residents on missions, Aboriginal people were considered ineligible for unemployment benefits as they were considered to be in training or not looking for work.

The Racial Discrimination Commissioner's Report on the Community Development Employment Program (CDEP) and racial discrimination tells us that: 'In the case of Indigenous people working on pastoral properties, the station managers were routinely reimbursed by the Department of Social Security for their "maintenance" as they were considered "government dependants". For many Indigenous people up until the mid-1970s, the only income support benefit available was the training allowance. Full, effective access to social security benefits did not occur until the late 1970s and in some remote communities not until the early 1980s.

The Arbitration Commission decision that Aborigines should receive equal wages to those of white employees on pastoral properties came into effect on 1 December 1968. Many station owners could not or would not pay their Aboriginal workers equal wages and many Aborigines were forced off the stations that had been their homes for several generations (Human Rights and Equal Opportunity Commission, *The CDEP Scheme and Racial Discrimination: A report by the race discrimination commissioner*, December 1997, pp. 12–14; in the historical account of social security provision in Australia, the report cites Roe, J. (ed.), *Social Policy in Australia: Some perspectives 1901–1975*, Castille, Sydney, 1976; North Australia Development Unit, *Where to Now: The Department of Social Security payments and the Aboriginal and Torres Strait Islander communities in North Australia*, NACU research paper, Darwin, 1990, p. 12).

5   With older Aboriginal communities such as in Redfern in inner Sydney or in the western suburbs of Sydney growing quickly with the rural influx, and new communities of Aboriginal people springing up, such as in Inala in Brisbane, Aboriginal organisations were developed to service these highly disadvantaged people. Aboriginal rights were supported by a growing urban non-Indigenous population, and young doctors and lawyers volunteered in the fledging cooperatives that emerged in shopfronts to provide urgently needed services. The model of the 'community-controlled' Aboriginal medical and legal services quickly spread across the country and resulted in a form of popular Aboriginal governance, that, while largely concerned with service delivery, nevertheless provided a social and political form of association that empowered Aboriginal communities in their dealings with governments and with neighbouring non-Indigenous populations.

6   For the next quarter of a century, this question was debated in a special forum in the United Nations, convened to consider the circumstances of 'Indigenous Populations'. The Working Group on Indigenous Populations was formed in 1982 and later the UN Permanent Forum on Indigenous Issues was established in 2000. On 13 September 2007, the General Assembly of the United Nations adopted the UN Declaration on the Rights of Indigenous Peoples, which sets out the individual and collective rights of the world's 370 million native peoples, calls for the maintenance and

strengthening of their cultural identities, and emphasises their right to pursue development in keeping with their own needs and aspirations. The Declaration is a non-binding text and enshrines standards. The final count of votes was: 143 in favour to four against (Australia, Canada, New Zealand and the United States), with eleven abstentions. After the election at which Prime Minister John Howard lost his seat and his government, Australia agreed to the Declaration.

7   The very high Aboriginal mortality rates, especially in remote regions, results in much shorter periods per generation than for the rest of the population. An Aboriginal generation can be as short as fifteen years where mortality rates are very high.

8   The Northern Territory, the poorest of Australia's jurisdictions, is heavily dependent on Commonwealth funding rather than its own tax base. For example, 'GST grants account for 33 per cent of State budget revenues, with the percentages for individual states varying from 25 per cent for WA to 69 per cent for the Northern Territory,' (Berry, C., 'Horizontal Fiscal Equalisation and Regional Development', http://epubs.scu.edu.au/jesp/vol14/iss3/6/, p. 2).

The Northern Territory is especially dependent on the Commonwealth's 'Indigenous Affairs' budget transfers as both general purpose grants and 'untied grants'. The untied grants are just that. They involve no Commonwealth or parliamentary oversight and the expenditure; even if it was intended for the Indigenous population to overcome disadvantage, it is often redirected to other purposes. Northern Territory governments have traditionally subsidised the high standards of living of the non-Indigenous population in Darwin's northern suburbs from these Commonwealth transfers. The large and relatively poor Aboriginal population attracts the highest rate of all jurisdictions of Commonwealth subsidy of services via the Commonwealth Grants Commission determination of horizontal fiscal equalisation. The Commonwealth distributes taxation revenues to the states and territories (one of the principal purposes of our Constitution) on the basis of horizontal fiscal equalisation. (See www.budget.gov.au/1997-98/horizont.asp for further explanation; also www.aph.gov.au/Parliamentary_Business/Committees/Senate_Committees?url=reffed_ctte/reffed/report/c05.htm, and Ross Garnaut and Vince Fitzgerald, Issues in Commonwealth-State Funding: www.rossgarnaut.com.au/Documents/Issues%20in%20Commonwealth-State%20Funding%20AFR%202002.pdf

THREE Legacies, new partnerships and plans: How traditional owners can settle their grievances with the old mining culture

1 Vice-President Paul Wand developed the policy after consulting with many Aboriginal people. See, for instance, the account by Associate Professor R. Howitt, who has studied the history of CRA and Rio Tinto, in *Recognition, Respect and Reconciliation: Steps towards decolonisation?*, School of Earth Sciences, Macquarie University, NSW, September 1997, at URL, www.es.mq.edu.au/rhowitt/IAG98R.htm, Accessed 5 October 2012.

2 When the resource in the original mining lease area has been extracted and further ore bodies are located in the vicinity, companies apply for leases over these areas. In cases in which the mining operations commenced before 1994 when the *Native Title Act* commenced, the original leases may have required no agreement with the local traditional owners, depending on the jurisdiction. In the Northern Territory, an agreement under the *Aboriginal Land Rights (Northern Territory) Act (1976)* may have been settled if the operations

commenced after 1976. Since 1994, however, all applications for mining leases must pass the various tests of the *Native Title Act* as 'future acts,' and this may involve an agreement where native title rights and interests are determined, or where a claim has been registered, or where, as in the case of the Argyle Diamond Mine, despite there being no requirement to negotiate an agreement, the company chooses to do so because of corporate social responsibility and 'social licence to operate' policies.

3   In the Comalco case, it was appropriate that the premier apologise for the events in the 1950s at Mapoon, and elsewhere in the area in the subsequent four decades before the Indigenous Land Use Agreement was settled, because it was the Queensland government that was culpable for the actions of the police who burnt the houses and church at Mapoon, shot the dogs and removed the population in 1957. There were other outrages as well, but none were directly attributable to the company, while the executive actions of the Queensland government were blatant.

4   Galarrwuy Yunupingu, 'Serious Business', speech delivered at the University of Melbourne Law School, 26 October 2007, copy in possession of the author.

5   *Milirrpum v Nabalco Pty Ltd and the Commonwealth* (1971) 17 FLR 141.

6   *Milirrpum v Nabalco Pty Ltd and the Commonwealth* (1971) 17 FLR 10: 267.

7   See, for instance, *Johnson v. McIntosh* (1823) 21 US 54; *Worcester v. Georgia* (1832) 31 US 515; *Mitchell v. United States* (1935) 34 US 711; *Calder v. Attorney-General (British Columbia)* (1973) 34 DLR (3d) 145; Re Southern Rhodesia [1919] AC 211; *Amodu Tijani v. Secretary, Southern Nigeria* [1921] 2 AC 399 at 407.

8   In that case, it is not well understood that when Rio Tinto Ltd acquired the Jabiluka interest and mining lease (along

with many other projects across several industries) when the company purchased North Ltd, the company executives negotiated an agreement with the traditional owners to close the Jabiluka project until such time as the traditional owners agree to its being opened again. It is perhaps deliberate on the part of the 'wilderness' campaigners to conceal this outcome negotiated by the traditional owners.

FOUR The first Australians' gift to the world: 30 million hectares of protected areas to conserve environments and biodiversity

1   See Langton, M., *Burning Questions*, Centre for Indigenous Natural and Cultural Resource Management, Northern Territory University, Darwin, 1994.

2   Tim Flannery, *Quarterly Essay: After the future, Australia's new extinction crisis*, Black Inc., 2012, p. 33.

3   As I pointed out in an endnote in the Introduction, Professor Flannery said he had been misunderstood. "In writing that national parties are not 'safe', I meant that they are not secure as a permanent part of the national parks estate. I expressed no view whether biodiversity would be more or less secure under indigenous management … biodiversity has done best where NGOs and indigenous groups have worked," he said. *Sydney Morning Herald*, 8 December 2013.

4   Until recently, approval for resource extraction activities, such as fracking, near non-Aboriginal residential areas would not have been contemplated by governments. The approvals for mining activities in remote Australia, especially on former Aboriginal reserves, and the disregard for impacts on Aboriginal people in previous decades reveal the Australian traditions of racism towards Aboriginal people. Now, though, non-Indigenous Australians, such as the members of agricultural and grazing industry associations – many of whom abused Aboriginal people for their objections to

mining – are faced with similar treatment by governments in relation to fracking and coal seam gas approvals, and yet have not noticed the irony of this history and their part in it.

5   See Rigsby, B., 'Aboriginal people, land rights, and wilderness on Cape York Peninsula', in Proceedings of the Royal Society of Queensland, 92, 1981, pp. 1–10; see also 'Aboriginal, people, land tenure and National Parks', in *Proceedings of the Royal Society of Queensland*, 106 (Pt 2), pp. 11–15; Guy, K., 'Development and conservation in Queensland: Environmental racism?' in *Perspectives on Indigenous Peoples' Management of Environment Resources: Ecopolitics IX conference papers and resolutions*, Northern Land Council, Casuarina, Darwin, 1996, pp. 108–112.

6   Aboriginal Land Fund Commission, *Koowarta v. Bjelke-Petersen* (1982) 153 CLR 168, paragraph 2; also cited by Collings, N., 'The Wik: A history of their 400 year struggle', in *Indigenous Law Bulletin*, no. 11, 1997: www.austlii.edu.au/au/journals/ILB/1997/29.html#fn26

7   As cited by Collings, ibid.; see also, Hanks, P.J., *Australian Constitutional Law: Materials and commentary*, (4th ed.), Butterworths, Sydney, 1990, p. 6.

8   Aboriginal Land Fund Commission, *Koowarta v. Bjelke-Petersen* (1982) 153 CLR 168, paragraph 2.

9   See Parliament of Victoria, Federal–State Relations Committee, *Report on International Treaty Making and the Role of the States* at www.parliament.vic.gov.au/fsrc/report1/body/Chapter2.htm#ch2sub1

10 In Australia's Northern Territory, for example, Aboriginal people own over 50 per cent of the land mass and over 80 per cent of the coastline. The lands and waters that constitute most of this area are not subject to high-density settlement, degradation of natural values by industries such as agriculture,

forestry, fishing, pastoralism and tourism, and are high-integrity areas both in terms of so-called natural and cultural values. Much of the lands and waters within the Indigenous domain remain subject to Indigenous management systems. Indigenous people are also an increasing proportion of rural and remote communities, with a birth rate higher than the rest of the Australian population. See Langton, M. "The 'Wild', the Market, and the Native: Indigenous People Face New forms of Global Colonization." In Globalization, Globalism, Environments, and Environmentalism. Consciousness of Connections, The Linacre Lectures, edited by S. Vertovec and D. Posey, Oxford University Press, 2003. pp. 141–167

11   *Mabo and Others v. Queensland* (No. 2) (1992) 175 CLR 1.

12   Under Australian law, native title may be recognised in areas of unalienated Crown land where Indigenous people continue to follow their traditional laws and customs and have maintained a link with their traditional country. These criteria pose severe obstacles for those Indigenous Australians who have in the past been forcibly removed from their lands. See Maureen Tehan, 'A Hope Disillusioned an Opportunity Lost? Reflections on Common Law Native Title and Ten Years of the Native Title Act' 27 (2) Melbourne University Law Review 523, 529–532.

13   In an appeal by Aboriginal activist Marandoo Yanner in relation to his charge under Queensland's *Fauna Conservation Act 1974* for hunting crocodiles; see *Yanner v. Eaton* (1999) HCA 53.

14   See Hassall & Associates, *Evaluation of the NHT Phase 1 Facilitator, Coordinator and Community Support Networks*, report prepared for Environment Australia and Commonwealth Department of Agriculture, Fisheries, Forestry, 2003, p. 100. For example, ongoing commercial

purchases by the Indigenous Land Corporation and Aboriginal Land Councils. The Australian Indigenous Land Corporation (ILC) operates under the *Native Title Act 1993* to fund land acquisition and land management activities. The ILC may undertake land management activities on all Indigenous-held land, including lands it has assisted Indigenous peoples to acquire. For land to be classified as 'Indigenous-held land', it must be held by an 'Indigenous organisation'. Land ownership, and support for the management of that land, is thus legitimised by the administrative category of an 'Indigenous organisation'. These benefits include the employment/training of Indigenous people and Indigenous business development.

15 See for example Lawrence, D., 'Managing Parks/Managing Country: Joint management of Aboriginal owned protected areas in Australia', research paper no. 2 1996–1997, Department of the Parliament Library, Canberra, 1996; *Kakadu: The making of a national park*, The Miegunyah Press, Melbourne University Press, Carlton, 2000; Palmer, L., 'Fishing Lifestyles: "Territorians', traditional owners and the management of recreational fishing in Kakadu National Park', *Australian Geographical Studies*, vol. 42, no. 1, 2004, pp. 60–76; Power, T., 'Joint Management at Uluru-Kata Tjuta National Park', *Environmental and Planning Law Journal*, vol. 19, no. 4, 2002, pp. 284–302.

16 I am indebted to Dr L. Palmer and Dr Z. Ma Rhea for permission to use work published originally in Langton, M., Ma Rhea, Z., & Palmer, L., 'Community Oriented Protected Areas for Indigenous Peoples and Local Communities: A study of developments Australasia', *Journal of Political Ecology*, vol. 12, 2005, pp. 23–49.

17 Commonwealth of Australia, *The National Strategy for the Conservation of Australia's Biological Diversity*,

Commonwealth Department of Environment, Sport and
Territories, Canberra, 1996, p. 9.
18   Smyth, D. &. Sutherland, J., *Indigenous Protected Areas:
     Conservation partnerships with Indigenous landholders*,
     Environment Australia, Canberra, 1996, pp. 96–97.
19   Ibid.
20   Smyth, D., *Protecting Country – Indigenous Protected Areas
     Phase Two Report*, consultancy report prepared for the
     Australian Nature Conservation Agency, Canberra, 1995.
21   Correspondence between Dr Lisa Palmer and the late S.
     Szabo 2002.
22   The analysis here relates not only to the cases settled
     between 1996 and 2005, but also to the additional
     Indigenous Protected Areas concluded since then. See www.
     environment.gov.au/indigenous/ipa/index.html.
23   See for example, Muller, S., 'Towards Decolonisation of
     Australia's Protected Area Management: The Nantawarrina
     Indigenous Protected Area experience', *Australian
     Geographical Studies*, vol. 41 no.1, 2003, pp. 29–43.
24   However, at present, Indigenous Protected Areas offer only
     short-term funding contracts, so that Indigenous land
     management organisations must constantly seek ongoing and
     additional sources of funding. Average annual funding from
     the Department of Environment and Heritage to each IPA is
     A$110,000 per annum.
25   Robertson, M., Vang, K. & Brown, A.J., *Wilderness in
     Australia: Issues and options. A discussion paper*, written
     for the Minister for the Arts, Sport, the Environment and
     Territories, Australian Heritage Commission, Canberra,
     1992, p. xi.
26   Flannery, T., *The Future Eaters: An ecological history of the
     Australasian lands and people*, Reed, NSW, 1994.

FIVE The new narrative of Indigenous success

1   Two clauses pertaining to 'race' remain in the Australian
     Constitution and enable racial discrimination by the
     Commonwealth Government. They are Section 51 (xxvi) and
     Section 25. To read more about the Constitution, see www.
     youmeunity.org.au.

2   Hughes, R., *The Culture of Complaint: The fraying of America*,
     Oxford University Press, New York/Oxford, 1993.

3   Windschuttle, K., *The Fabrication of Aboriginal History*,
     Macleay Press, Sydney, 2009.

4   Sandall, R., *The Culture Cult: Designer tribalism & other
     essays*, Perseus Books Group, Westview Boulder, Colo:
     2001. Sandall's attack on what he calls the 'culture cult'
     is not recommended reading, but for those who want to
     know more, I provide a few excerpts. His attack is twofold:
     first, he savages those modern white folk who hold positive
     views about cultural relativism; and second, he proves
     them 'wrong' with an unrelentingly racist diatribe against
     Indigenous people and non-whites. His main proposition (the
     'Pocahontas syndrome') is that cultural relativists hold three
     dogmas unquestionable:

     ... 1. each culture is a semisacred creation, 2. all cultures
     are equally valuable and must never be compared, and 3.
     the assimilation of cultures (especially the assimilation
     of primitive cultures by a secular civilisation coldly
     indifferent to spiritual things) is supremely wicked [page
     89].

     He rebukes these alleged views – which he regards as
     treachery to their own grand white 'civilisation', with
     passages such as the following:

     ... knowledge of what was stagnant, miserable, cruel,
     and absurd about the old way of life is suppressed.
     Replacing it is a genteel upside-down version of the past

– a vision of native tradition which is domesticated and innocuous, where peace and smiling happiness prevail, where spirituality flourishes and the gods are kind. Unsurprisingly, the heirs of tribalism enthusiastically approve this new and academically authorized version of their lives[page 180].

… When Cook and others meet the axe-and-club wielding indigenes of the South Pacific, men are killed on both sides, but they are baked and eaten by one side only [page 179].

… Maori traditions would be idealized beyond recognition. With not a battle or broken head in sight, let alone cannibal feasts, their culture would be portrayed as something that had been tragically 'taken from them' like the land itself. This dual expropriation would then be used to explain every imaginable failing, Colonial history would be rewritten as a purely oral drama of villains and victimhood … the moral superiority of the oppressed [page 121].

… Illiterate, vocationally disabled, unpresentable outside the ethnographic zoos they live in, these tragic people are Australia's contribution to the New Stone Age [page 17].

5   Noel Pearson, Executive Director, Cape York Land Council, 'Indigenous People and International Law', Address to the Evatt Foundation Annual Dinner, Friday 28 July 1995. Copy in possession of the author.

6   Ben Wyatt, Report on Speech to the Indigenous Business and Economic Development Conference, University of Western Australia, www.news.uwa.edu.au/201212045318/events/ education-seen-key-indigenous-regional-empowerment

See also www.business.uwa.edu.au/ibecconference/__data/ assets/pdf_file/0007/2242177/Session-3.1-Web.pdf; author's notes

www.ingramcontent.com/pod-product-compliance
Lightning Source LLC
Chambersburg PA
CBHW032144020426
42334CB00016B/1219